Basic Office English

A. Ashley

Pitman

PITMAN PUBLISHING LIMITED
128 Long Acre, London WC2E 9AN

A Longman Group Company

© A. Ashley, 1986

First published in Great Britain, 1986

British Library Cataloguing in Publication Data

Ashley, A.
    Basic office English.
    1. English language—Text-books for
    foreign speakers   2. English language—
    Business English
    I. Title
    808'.066651021   PE1128

ISBN 0-273-02409-4

Printed and bound in Great Britain at The Bath Press, Avon.

Contents

Introduction

Basic Office English is an essential book for students of office practice who are learning English as a second or foreign language at intermediate or advanced levels. However, it is also recommended for those whose first language is English but would like an introduction into office procedures and want to strengthen their knowledge of the language in the context of business English, and therefore, the book takes into account changes in the language which have been influenced by the development of business technology.

Students will be introduced to office skills and practice so they will become familiar with the structure of companies, the ways they work, their correspondence, documents, and equipment, and the company's role in the commercial world.

The units cover the basic requirements for students following courses which lead to the London Chamber of Commerce, RSA, B. Tec, and Vocational Preparation examinations and have been designed to be used either as a classroom aid or by students working on their own. Each unit is tested by a series of relevant exercises either testing the students' knowledge of the practice or procedure, or language skill, through dialogues, comprehensions, multiple choice, and cloze tests.

The book has been written with an instructional bias so that teachers and students with little or no business experience will easily follow the topic dealt with. Teachers particularly can adapt the content and exercises to class, group, or pair work to develop their students' structural and communicative skills by expanding on grammar and usage points, and setting up role plays based on the issues raised in the dialogues and contents of the units.

For those interested in the wider aspects of the commercial and business world, there is also *Basic Commercial English* and *A Handbook of Commercial Correspondence* (Oxford University Press) by the same author.

UNIT 1

Finding a job

1.1 Advertisements

There are a number of different ways people find jobs. Friends or relatives might tell them that their company needs someone for a particular position, or government or private agencies who specialise in 'job finding' could help. Some people write directly to companies to ask if there are vacancies even if a post has not been advertised. Most people, however, find a job through advertisements in newspapers or magazines through the **situations vacant** columns.

Usually the adverts are abbreviated, so that **salary per month** becomes **sal. p.m.** and **three weeks holiday a year** could be written **3 wks. hol. p.y.** or **p.a.** for per annum. The three examples below, however, are written out in full.

Exercise 1

'What did they say?'
Once you have read the advertisements carefully, answer the questions.

General clerical assistant

Large department store requires general clerical assistant, 16–19 years old, to work in Accounts Department. No experience required, but must like working with figures and be willing to help with general duties when necessary.

We are an expanding company and there are prospects for advancement after a one year training period.

There is a good starting salary with three weeks paid annual leave. Hours 9.00–5.00 Monday to Friday. Subsidised staff canteen and staff discount.

Apply in writing to:

Mr. L M Green
Personnel Manager
UK Stores Ltd.
1–10 Great Russell Street
London WC1

(a)

NATIONAL OIL

The National Oil Company PLC
Burmah House
35 Kallang Pudding Road
Singapore 13 34
(Phone: 6651481/2/3/4)

Clerk/typist, male or female, to work in large modern office handling correspondence, 'phone, filing, and general duties.
Typing 40 words per minute. Some experience preferred so should be familiar with office routine.
Age: 16–19
Hours: 09.00 – 17.00
Annual increments and staff bonus. Luncheon vouchers. Non-contributory pension scheme. After a one year period, we will allow half-day release a week to follow office practice or business studies course at a recognised college of further education.
Apply in writing or by phone to (Mrs) D. Chan, Personnel Officer for application form.

(b)

Advance Advertising

Advance Advertising (Lagos) is looking for a bright lively person who will be willing to help out in busy agency. One day you may be in the post-room, the next delivering urgent parcels, or helping our Director fix an appointment. You will be busy and may have to work late or on week-ends but you will get a lot of experience in a small agency. Interested? Then call us at 416–513, or 416–810, and ask for Mary Alabi in personnel.

(c)

1 Which advertisement asked for experience?
2 Did any of the advertisements ask for particular qualifications?
3 One advert talked about the applicant's character. How did they say this?
4 How did advert (a) explain the company offered a 'career'?
5 Which would you think was the most relaxed, or least formal company to work for?
6 What could be the disadvantages in working for the advertising company in (c)?
7 One of the advantages of working for The National Oil Company was that they offered a 'non-contributory pension scheme', which meant that after their staff retired – stopped work at about 60 – they would be paid part of their salary

and they did not have to pay anything towards this while they were working (non-contributory). What other benefits did this company offer?

8 Did the advertising agency want the applicant to write to them to apply for the job?

9 What phrase did the department store in (a) use to say they wanted someone who 'liked accounts'?

10 In some countries it is against the law to say a company wants either a man or woman to do a particular job.

What phrases were used in the three adverts to explain either a man or woman could apply?

Exercise 2

Vocabulary

1 In the first paragraph of this Unit there were four words used for 'job'. What were they?

2 Which word replaced 'wages' in the advertisements?

3 Which word was used to explain that the company would help pay for staff meals in (a)?

4 Which word was used in (b) to mean 'writing letters'?

5 Two expressions were used to mean 'yearly'. What were they?

6 The expression 'bank holidays' was used to explain that the company in (b) gave days off when the banks were closed. They could also have said 'public holidays'. What other words were used instead of 'holidays'?

7 What did the words 'negotiable' and 'increments' mean in (b)?

8 In (b) what word did they use for 'general office procedure'?

9 In (a) what was used to explain there was a 'future' with the company?

10 Which word could be used instead of 'publicity'?

Exercise 3

Abbreviations

We said that advertisements are often abbreviated. The abbreviations in **bold** type below can all be found in the three examples. Explain what they mean.

Large **Co.** requires **clk/typ** as **asst.** to **accnts mngr.,** and to help with **gen.** duties. **Sal.** $6000 **p.a.** 3 **wks. vac. p.a.** 5 day **p.w. Hrs.** 9.00–5.00. **L.Vs. Tel.** 01 345 1171.

1.2 Applying for a job

You could apply for a job by going to the company in person if the advertisement asked you to 'call round'. The example of (c) asked applicants to 'phone' them. Generally, though, most companies will ask you to 'write' to them.

The letter might only ask them to send you an **application form** which you fill out giving information about yourself (see fig. 1). Or the letter may have to include all the details about yourself and be sent with a **curriculum vitae**, abbreviated to **cv**, which is an information sheet that you write out describing your qualifications and career so far. However, even if you only send an 'accompanying letter' or 'covering letter' with the application form, you might have to explain some details that are not clear, or simply tell the company you are returning the completed form and hope they will offer you an interview.

The example below is the sort of 'covering letter' that might be sent to the oil company who advertised in (c), along with their application form.

```
APPLICATION FORM FOR:              THE NATIONAL OIL CO. PLC
                                   Burmah House, 35 Kallang Pudding Road
DATE:                              Singapore 13 34   Tel: 6651481/2/3/4

FOR THE POST OF:        DEPARTMENT:              REFERENCE:

FAMILY NAME:                    FORENAME(S):

ADDRESS:      street       city       district

PHONE: (Home)                  (Work)

DATE OF BIRTH:        AGE:       BIRTHPLACE:

STATUS: Married/Single      MAIDEN NAME:

DEPENDENTS:            NEXT OF KIN (Name and Address)

                                              Recent Photo

EDUCATION:  Secondary with names of school(s) and Principal(s)
                        FROM   TO   EXAMINATIONS taken or to be taken
                                                         Grade Year

FURTHER EDUCATION:  Principal(s)   Addresses   Type of Course
                        FROM   TO   EXAMINATIONS taken or to be taken
                                                         Grade Year

PREVIOUS EMPLOYMENT:  Names of companies and managers/supervisors
                        FROM   TO   POST & DUTIES    Reasons for leaving

Please indicate if you have had experience with the following:

Typing .... w.p.m.    Shorthand .... w.p.m.    Computers (Type) ....

Clerical ....          Correspondence ....      Filing ....

Accounts (to what level?) ....    Post room .... Driving Licence ....


HOBBIES & SPORTS

Please give a brief statement as to why you are applying for this
position:


REFERENCES:      (a)  Name:                   Address:

                 (b)  Name:                   Address:

Signed ..................           Date:
```

Fig. 1 Application form

Covering letter

```
                                              House Road / Street
                                              District
                                              Area / Postal Code

                                              Date

       The Personnel Officer
       The National Oil Co. PLC
       35 Kallang Pudding Road
       Singapore 13 34


       Dear Mrs. Chan,

       Thank you for sending me the application form for the post of
       clerk/typist which I 'phoned for last Monday.
       I have now completed the form and am returning it with this
       letter.  If there is any further information you need, please
       contact me.

       Yours sincerely,

       Name  (signed)

       Full name  (typed)
```

```
                          CURRICULUM VITAE

       NAME:  Kim Lam (Miss)              DATE:  5th July 19..

       ADDRESS:  53 Southport Road        PHONE:  (Home) 01 573 6734
                 London E15 1EF

       AGE:  19     PLACE OF BIRTH:  Hong Kong   NATIONALITY:  British

       APPLICATION FOR:  General Clerical Assistant
                         UK Stores Ltd.

       EDUCATION:  Kowloon College 19.. to 19..

       EXAMS TAKEN:  School Leaving Certificate   DATE:  June 19..

       SUBJECTS AND GRADES:

       Mandarin (B);  English (B);  Mathematics (C);  Geography (C);
       Commerce (B);  Accounts (B).

       FURTHER EDUCATION:  Leyton Further Education College 19.. to 19..

       EXAMS TAKEN:  B.TEC. National Certificate  DATE:  June 19..

       SUBJECTS AND GRADES:

       Business Studies       (Still awaiting results)

       SKILLS:  Typing 35 w.p.m. Electric and Manual machines

       INTERESTS:  Volleyball;  fashion;  pop music;  films

       REFERENCES:

       Mrs. W. Peng MA, Head, Kowloon College, To Kwan Road, Kowloon.

       Mr. D. Levy MA BSc, Principal, Leyton Further Education College
                         Leyton, London E15 1EG
```

Fig. 2 Curriculum vitae

Curriculum vitae (abbreviation cv)

Sometimes the advertisements ask for a **curriculum vitae** (cv) to be sent with a letter. This is an application form that you yourself design. There is no particular way of writing a cv, but the information should be given in a form which answers questions which an employer would most likely ask first, second, third, and so on.

Look at how the information is presented by Kim Lam, in fig. 2. She is replying to advertisement (a) which asked for a 'general clerical assistant'.

Along with her cv, Kim will send the following letter:

---

53 Southport Road [1]

London E15 1EF

[2]
The Personnel Manager   5th July 19..
UK Stores Ltd
1-10 Great Russell Street
London WC1

[3]
Dear Mr Green,

I would like to apply for the position of 'general clerical assistant' which you advertised in 'The Daily News' on 3rd July 19..

As you will see from the enclosed cv I am 19 years old, Chinese, but with British Nationality, and I have just left Leyton F.E. College where I was studying a business course.

My family moved from Hong Kong to London two years ago and as we have now settled in London I would like to find a permanent position here with a large company which offers prospects of advancement.

The post and conditions you advertised interest me as I would like to study accounts and I am very interested in the retail trade.

I think my business studies and willingness to learn will be useful to your company, and I hope you can offer me a chance to attend an interview where I can give you more information about myself.

I look forward to hearing from you,

[4] Yours sincerely,

Kim Lam

[5] Kim Lam (Miss)

Fig. 3 Letter applying for a job

1.3 Layout of letters of application

The layout of letter usually follows the style Kim Lam used in fig. 3.

Addresses

Addresses should be written in full with area or district codes, and if the letter is going abroad the name of the country should be added.

The **writer's address** is put on the top right[1] with the date a few spaces below it. The **receiver's address** with his/her name or title goes on the left in line with the date, or a line or so below it[2], and it is better to put dates in full, rather than just figures as 3.10.86 appears as 10th March 1986 to many countries, and 3rd October 1986 to other countries like the UK.

In modern letters addresses are not punctuated with commas at the end of each line, but if you are going to punctuate make sure you put the commas and stops on every line. Abbreviations, however, should be punctuated with stops, e.g. J.R. Robinson & Co. Ltd. – J.R. Robinson and Company Limited. Sometimes stops are left out when letters represent the name of an organisation or an expression, for example the East African Federation, or the United Nations Organisation will appear as EAF, or UNO rather than E.A.F. or U.N.O. In the advertisement we saw for The National Oil Company, the letters PLC followed the company's name. This means **public limited company**. The word **limited** (Ltd.) shows that the company has limited responsibility if it goes bankrupt – fails to pay all its debts – and PLC means the company is **public** – the general public can buy shares in it.

Salutations

In the UK letters are opened with **Dear Sir,** or **Dear Madam,** followed by a comma, if the receiver's name is not known. If you do know the person's name then **Dear Mr. Smith,** or Dear Miss (unmarried), Mrs. (married), Ms. (no status) Smith, is used, again followed by a comma. Look at how Kim opened her letter[3].

The body of the letter – paragraphs

The main part of the letter will be in paragraphs which are separated by one or two space lines. As a general guide, a paragraph deals with a subject or related subjects – in other words 'an idea' or 'ideas which are linked to one another'.

In Kim's letter her first paragraph dealt with the reference to the advertisement, which lets the receiver know immediately what she is writing about. Her second paragraph referred to her cv, reminding the reader of the main points. The third explained why she was living in England and led into the fourth paragraph which told UK Stores why she wanted to work for them. In the final section she explained why she thought she would be suitable for the position and that she would like an interview.

Complimentary close – Yours faithfully,/Yours sincerely,

If you do not know the receiver's name and open with Dear Sir, or Dear Madam, then close with **Yours faithfully**. If you open with Dear Mr. Smith, or Dear Miss/Mrs./Ms./Smith, then close with **Yours sincerely**. Both forms are followed by a comma[4].

If you know someone quite well and are on first name terms with them, you can use **Best wishes**, or just **Regards**.

Finally, you should sign your name so that it can be read, as if typing the letter, type your full name and title below your signature[5], as Kim did in her letter.

Block and indented styles

Most modern letters are written in a **blocked style** with addresses and paragraphs all beginning at the margin. If the **indented style** is used, then follow it throughout the letter with addresses and paragraphs.

Block	Indented
The Sales Manager	The Personnel Manager
A & C Industries Ltd.	Barman's Bank Ltd.
Ikeja Industrial Layout	183-186 Boon Keng Road
Lagos	P.O. Box 8651
Nigeria	Singapore

Exercise 4

What are the 10 mistakes in this letter which was sent with an application form?

```
                                        Mr. L. Chang
                                           45 Bridge Road
                                           Hong Kong

        The Personnel Officer
        The Royal Insurance Co Ltd
        On Lok Yuen Building
        25 Des Voeux Road
        Central


        Dear Sir

        I would like to apply for the position of filing clerk.

        As you will see from my application form I've just left College
        and hope to get a post with an insurance company where there will
        be a chance of making a carrer, and the position you advertised
        seems to offer the opportunity I am looking for.

        I think my business studies course and ability to work hard and
        learn would be useful to your company.  I hope you can offer me
        an interview where I can give you more details about myself.

        I look forward to hear from you,

        Yours sincerely,

        L. Chang

        L. Chang
```

Exercise 5

From the following information about Vinard Patel, who is applying for a job as a 'filing clerk' with The National Oil Company of Singapore fill out the **application form on page 4,** fig. 1.

He is applying on July 15, 1986, and was.given FC/5 as a reference in the advertisement. He lives at 1123, Sims Avenue, Singapore, 1438, and his phone number is 7116398.

Vinard was born in 1970 in Singapore, he is not married and has no dependents and his mother Mrs. R. Patel, who he lives with, is his next of kin.

He was educated at the Merchant Secondary School in Raffles Road in Singapore from 1981 and has just left after taking School Leaving Certificate, but does not have his examination results yet. As he is only sixteen, he has not.had any further education or work experience, but he is interested in clerical work and thinks that the job offered will give him experience and is willing to take a business studies course at night school.

Mr. R. Davies, the headmaster of his school and Mrs. B. Trevedi, his commerce teacher will give him references.

He is a good swimmer, likes football and films, and sometimes goes to discos.

1.4 Guide to applying for a job

Although we call the letters we look at 'applications for jobs', they are really applications for **interviews**. Therefore, it would be worth looking at these points when writing a letter for a position.

(a) Open your letter by referring to the advertisement, and when and where you saw it. Remember that when we quote the name of a magazine or newspaper we use single **quotation** marks – 'The Singapore Times', or 'The Nigerian Daily News'. If someone recommended you, then tell the company – *Mr. J. Odinga, who works in your Accounts Department told me that you will soon have a vacancy for* . . . . If there is no advertisement or recommendation, then you can open your letter by writing –
I am writing to ask if you might have a vacancy in your Post Room/Accounts Department/Filing Department etc., then continue the letter as you would if there was an advertisement.

(b) If you are sending a cv or application form you can refer to it to mention any points you think need to be explained. But be brief as there will be a number of applications and the person you are writing to will not have time to read pages of written script.

(c) You should tell the company why you are interested in the job and what you think you can offer them. Look at how Kim Lam did this in her letter.

(d) You can close the letter by saying you look forward to an interview where you will give them further information, or you could tell them that if they need any more information immediately you will send it to them.

(e) As you are writing for an **interview**, and not a job, you should not discuss salary or conditions, as all this would be discussed at the interview itself.

(f) If you are already working for a company and want to change your employment, do not criticise the company you are working for. You can tell them that you want the new job as they are offering 'better prospects'; 'a chance to advance'; 'they will give you a chance to use your experience'; etc. And you should explain these reasons briefly in your letter.

(g) Writing in English is almost the same as speaking to someone, except you should not use contractions, e.g. I've worked, instead of **I have worked**, or **I'm studying** instead of **I am studying**. But apart from being more particular in our language when we write, written and spoken communication are almost the same.

If you just take the answers to the spoken questions below, you will see that you could build a letter from them:

Q: 'Why are you writing to us?'
A: 'I am writing to apply for the position advertised . . . .'
Q: 'Where did you go to school/college, and what have you done since then?'
A: 'I went to (name of school/college), from . . . to . . . , and then studied . . . and took/passed (examinations. I left school/college in . . . and began work with . . . etc.,
Q: 'Why do you think we should give you this job?'
A: 'I think my experience and studies would be useful to you because . . .
Q: 'Would you like an interview?'
A: 'I hope you can offer me an interview where I can give you more information about myself.'

Finally, your letter should be neat whether it is written or typed. Check your spellings, particularly of names. Do not cross out, but rewrite the letter. Remember, your application will be the only thing your employer knows about you, so there is no second chance.

Exercise 6

The following words have all been used in this unit, and are often mis-spelled. Choose the correct spelling from the two lists.

1	application	aplication	8	permanent	permanant
2	necessary	neccessary	9	adress	address
3	receive	recieve	10	acounts	accounts
4	clark	clerk	11	abbreviation	abreviation
5	sincerely	sincerly	12	personel	personnel
6	faithfuly	faithfully	13	assisstant	assistant
7	business	bussines	14	secondary	secondery

Exercise 7

The advertisement (c) (page 2 in this Unit) was placed by Advance Advertising (Lagos) in 'The Daily News'. With the information given below, explain on the phone that you are interested in the position as a general assistant and would like to apply for the job.

You are David Low, 17 years old, and finished secondary school last year with a School Leaving Certificate and have done a one year office practice course at your local technical college. The results of your RSA examinations will come through in two months' time.

You are interested in the advertising profession and would like to know more about the practical side of it by working for an agency. You do not mind working hard, or long hours and can attend an interview at any time.
Example: 'Could I have your name and age please?'
              '. . . David Low, . . . seventeen years old.'
Answer: **My name is** David Low, **and I'm** seventeen years old.'

SWITCHBOARD: 'Advance Advertising (Lagos)?'
YOU: 'I'd like . . . please, it's about . . . .'
SWITCHBOARD: 'One moment, I'll put you through. You are through to Miss Alabi, caller.'

MISS ALABI: 'Hallo, Mary Alabi speaking, can I help you?'
YOU: 'Good morning, my name is . . . , and I . . . .'
MISS ALABI: 'Could you give me some information about yourself?'
YOU: 'I am (age), and I live . . . , and have just finished . . . , where I . . . .'
MISS ALABI: 'Did you pass your RSA?'
YOU: 'I . . . , but I'm sure I passed them.'
MISS ALABI: 'Why are you applying for this job?'
YOU: 'I . . . .'
MISS ALABI: 'You understand the work will be varied and you'll be doing different jobs to help people out, and might have to work some evenings or weekends?'
YOU: 'Yes, but I . . . .'
MISS ALABI: 'When would you be available for an interview?'
YOU: 'I can . . . .'
MISS ALABI: 'That's fine. Would tomorrow afternoon at 2.30 suit you?'
YOU: '. . . .'
MISS ALABI: 'Our address is 451 Herbert Macaulay Street, Yaba, we are next door Barton's Stores, is that okay?'
YOU: 'Yes, I'll . . . .'
MISS ALABI: 'When you get here, go to reception and ask for me. I'll meet you there, then take you to Mr. Onokayo who'll interview you. Oh yes, could you bring your School Leaving Certificate with you?'
YOU: 'Yes, I'll do that.'
MISS ALABI: 'Good, we'll look forward to seeing you then, goodbye.'
YOU: 'Goodbye.'

1.5 Invitation to an interview

In Exercise 6 we saw that an interview could be arranged on the 'phone, but often interviews are arranged by letter. The letter in fig. 4 is from UK Stores asking Kim Lam to attend an interview.

Notice in this letter, fig. 4, that the company's address is heading the paper[1], and there are details on how to contact them by phone, telex, and cable[2]. There is also information about the company's registration number, as most British companies have to be registered with the Registrar of Companies, and there is a VAT number, which is the company's sales tax number[3].

At the very bottom of the page the Chairman – the senior executive of the company – and the Board of Directors – the other important executives – are also listed[8]. All this information must be given in the company's correspondence by law.

The reference on this letter, LMG/TW[4], indicates that it was sent by Leonard Green (LMG) and typed by his secretary, Terry White (TW). If Kim replies to this letter she should quote this reference. Sometimes there are figures with a reference, in this case, for example, they might have written LMG/TW/15, and the '15' could be the 15th letter they have sent to applicants, or it could be the number of their department. Whatever it means to the company, it allows them to refer to correspondence quickly.

There is also an underlined note between the salutation and the opening of the letter, explaining the subject of the correspondence – 'General clerical assistant'[5]. This informs the reader exactly what the correspondence concerns.

Finally, Terry White, a secretary, has written the letter 'on behalf of' Leonard Green, so she writes *pp,* which means *per pro* and is Latin for 'on behalf of'[6].

UK STORES LTD [1]

Phone: 01 356 9110		Reg. London 315113
Telex: 661703	1–10 Great Russell Street	
Cable: UKSTOR [2]	London WC1	VAT No. 21 35116 [3]

Ref: LMG/TW [4]   12th July 19..

Miss Kim Lam
53 Southport Road
London E15

Dear Miss Lam,

<u>General clerical assistant</u> [5]

Thank you for writing to us and sending your c.v. in connection with above post.

I am pleased to tell you that Mr. Green, our Personnel Manager, will be pleased to see you for an interview on Thursday, 25th July at 10.00 a.m.

When you arrive, could you please go to the staff entrance of the store in Bedford Way, and take the lift to the 9th floor where one of the staff will be able to direct you to my office.

Would you bring with you your qualifications and any references you have been given? If you do not have references at present, we will contact the people you suggested in your application form after your interview.

I am enclosing a map showing the most convenient bus and underground services to get here.

Please phone me on extension 1156 to confirm you will be able to attend the interview on the date I have given, and if that is not convenient, we will arrange another appointment.

Yours sincerely,

Terry White

Terry White (Miss) [6]
p.p. Leonard Green, Personnel Manager.   Encl. [7]

Chairman: Sir Geoffrey Alcott   Directors: D.W.James OBE, S.L.Carter ACCA [8]
                                           W.S.Rose FIA, M.L.Daner FRIS

Fig. 4 An invitation to an interview

The map, fig. 5, is the one that Terry White is sending to Kim Lam to help her get to the store. Notice in the letter the abbreviation *Encl*[8] which indicates that there is something enclosed with the correspondence.

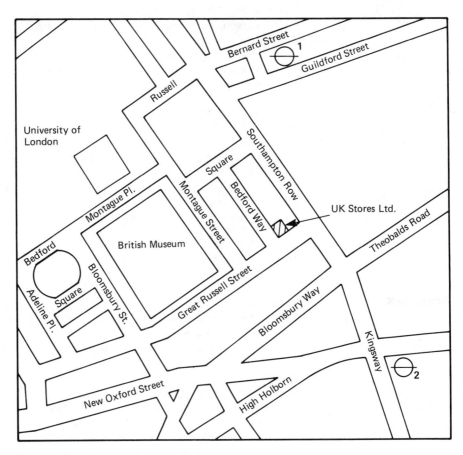

Fig. 5 A street map

Underground Stations:
1 Russell Square
   (Piccadilly Line)
2 Holborn
   (Northern and Central
   Lines)

Buses:
Nos 68, 77, and 188,
get off at stop after
Theobalds Road.

Trains – British Rail:
Euston and King's Cross/
St. Pancras
All in walking distance
of the store

Exercise 8

Kim is phoning to confirm that she will keep the appointment for the interview. Write what you think she would say in the conversation. Refer to the letter Terry White sent you.

Example: 'Which department do you want to speak to?'
              '. . . the sales department please.'
Answer: **'I'd like to speak to** the sales department please.'
SWITCHBOARD: 'UK Stores Limited:'
KIM: 'Can I . . . .'

SWITCHBOARD: 'Which department is that?'
KIM: '. . . .'
SWITCHBOARD: 'What extension?'
KIM: '. . . .'
SWITCHBOARD: 'Putting you through now.'
MISS WHITE: 'Personnel, extension 1156, Terry White here.'
KIM: 'My name is . . . and you . . . on . . . saying that I . . . with Mr. Leonard Green
the personnel manager, on . . . and I am phoning . . . on that date.'
MISS WHITE: 'One moment, I'm just looking for the letter. Did I give you a
reference?'
KIM: 'Yes, ...'
MISS WHITE: 'Yes, I've found it. So you can attend at 10.00 a.m. on the 25th?'
KIM: 'Yes.'
MISS WHITE: 'Good. From your address, it seems that it would be best to get the
Central Line Underground. Do you know which station to get out, and how to
walk down to here?'
KIM: 'Yes. I . . . at . . . , then walk up . . . , across . . . , then turn . . . into . . . and go
into the store through the . . · in . . . .'
MISS WHITE: 'D'you know which floor to come up to?'
KIM: 'It's . . . .'
MISS WHITE: 'Okay, Miss Lam, I look forward to seeing you then.'
KIM: 'Thank you, goodbye.'
MISS WHITE: ''Bye.'

Exercise 9

Conditionals

Complete the following sentences using the correct conditional.

Example: If companies **advertise**, . . . (sell)
         If companies advertise, they **will sell** their products

1   I think you would fail an interview, . . . (dress badly)
2   If your references are good, . . . (employ)
3   If you are late for the appointment, . . . (no interview)
4   Would you mind . . . ? (change interview date)
5   Unless you write clearly, . . . (not understand)
6   (leave early) . . . , you would not arrive on time.
7   If I knew their phone number, . . . (tell)
8   If you don't mind working late, . . . (offer the job)
9   (like working with figures) . . . , they will put him in the accounts department.
10   Unless you were willing to work hard, . . . (not apply)

1.6 Offering a job

Companies offer jobs by sending the applicant a letter congratulating them
on being successful at the interview. The letter will also confirm the terms
of employment that were discussed at the interview.

In fig. 6 Kim Lam has been offered the job she was interviewed for at UK
Stores Ltd. This too confirms the terms she discussed with the personnel
manager, Mr. Green. It states the hours she will work; what her duties will
be; her salary and annual rises; holidays and sick pay; and the 'fringe
benefits' the store offers – those benefits besides her salary – store discounts
and subsidised meals in the staff canteen.

Notice Kim will be required to **clock in**, and **clock off**, which means the
company has a machine with **time cards** that have to be marked in a clock
registering when staff begin and leave work (see fig. 7 as an example of a
clocking-in card).

UK STORES LTD

Phone: 01 356 9110
Telex: 661703
Cable: UKSTOR

1—10 Great Russell Street
London WC1

Reg. London 315113
VAT No. 21 35116

Ref: LMG/TW 2

30th July 19..

Miss Kim Lam
53 Southport Road
London E15

Dear Miss Lam,

<u>Appointment as General Clerical Assistant</u>

I am pleased to tell you that you were successful at your interview with Mr Green on 25 July, and we are offering you the above position to begin on Monday 15 September 19..

I would just like to confirm the conditions and terms that were agreed.

Your official hours will be from 9.00 a.m. to 5.00 p.m. Monday to Friday with one hour for lunch.

In the first year, your training year, your salary will be £4,524.00 with annual rises of 10 per cent for the next three years after that. If you are needed to do extra work, your overtime will be paid at time and a half for weekdays and double time for Sundays and Bank Holidays.

You will be allowed three weeks' annual paid vacation, plus the usual Public Holidays, and ten days a year paid sick leave, but you will have to provide a doctor's certificate if you are away for longer than any three days together.

Your immediate manager will be Mr. Alan Southern, and your duties will cover working the accounts section and helping out other sections when necessary.

As was explained to you, we have a clocking in and out system for all our staff with one hour's pay being added for every fifteen minutes in the hour you stay behind to work, and one hour being deducted for every fifteen minutes in the hour you are late.

You may use the staff canteen where subsidized meals are provided, the sports facilities of the store, and staff can buy any goods sold in the store at a 15 per cent discount.

Enclosed you will find two copies of your 'contract of employment', would you sign one and return it to me with a letter confirming that you accept the position?

I look forward to seeing you on Monday 15 September at 8.30 am when you will be introduced to your colleagues.

I am sure you will enjoy working here,

Yours sincerely,

Terry White

Terry White (Miss)
pp Leonard Green, Personnel Manager

Encls:
2 contracts of employment

Chairman: Sir Geoffrey Alcott   Directors: D.W.James OBE, S.L.Carter ACCA
W.S.Rose FIA, M.L.Daner FRIS

Fig. 6 A letter of appointment

The letter also reminds Kim that if she works more than her agreed hours – overtime – she will be paid at a higher rate. On the other hand, if she comes in late, pay will be deducted.

She has also been sent two copies of a 'Contract of Employment' which officially confirms the terms of her employment. She keeps one copy, and signs the other and returns it with her confirmation that she accepts the position.

Exercise 10

Choose the correct term. They are based on the letter UK Stores sent to Kim Lam.
1 Kim will have to (a) **clock on** (b) **clock off** (c) **clock out**/every morning
2 Her meals will be (a) **free** (b) **subsidised** (c) **expensive** in the staff canteen
3 She must (a) **keep her contracts of employment** (b) **return one copy, signed** (c) **return both copies, signed**
4 She will get (a) **three wage rises in her first year** (b) **one wage rise during her first year** (c) **three wage rises after her first year**
5 Kim will get (a) **ten days vacation** (b) **three weeks vacation** (c) **three days vacation**/per annum
6 She will work directly for (a) **Mr. Green** (b) **Miss White** (c) **Mr. Southern**
7 Her annual salary will be (a) **£4,050** (b) **£4,005** (c) **£4,524**
8 If she works overtime during the week, she will be paid (a) **double time** (b) **time and a half** (c) **half the time**
9 If she bought something in the store for £1.00 (which is 100 pence) she would pay (a) **95 pence** (b) **85 pence** (c) **75 pence**
10 Kim begins her job on the (a) **30 July** (b) **15 September** (c) **25 July**

Exercise 11

Here is the letter Kim sends back to UK Stores accepting the appointment. Put in the missing **prepositions**.

```
                                        53 Southport·Road
                                        London E15

                                        2nd August 19..

    Miss T. White
    Personnel Dept.
    UK Stores Ltd.
    1-10 Great Russell Street
    London WC1


    Dear Miss White,

    Thank you ... offering me the position ... General Clerical
    Assistant ... UK Stores Ltd.

    I would like to confirm that I accept the post and the conditions
    stated ... your letter ... 30 July which you sent ... me.

    I am enclosing one signed copy ... the Contract ... Employment,
    and I look forward ... seeing you ... Monday 15th September ...
    your office ... 8.30 a.m.

    Yours sincerely,

    Kim Lam

    Kim Lam (Miss)
```

1.7 Working conditions

```
UK Stores Ltd.                 CLOCK CARD              Staff No. 613/5
Name: Kim Lam
Week Ending: 23 Sept 19..                             Week No. 21
```

Day	In	Out	In	Out	TOTAL HOURS
M	0901	1305	1401	1706	7.09
Tu	0900	1302	1402	1702	7.02
W	0854	1304	1403	1704	7.11
Th	0903	1305	1401	1803	8.08
F	0856	1303	1404	1801	8.04
					37.34

Weekly Hrs...35...   Rate £ 87.00 p.w.   £ 87.00

£ 2.41 p.h.

Overtime @ 1½ ...2..., hrs. £ 3.63   7.26

TOTAL GROSS WAGES 94.26

Fig. 7 A clock card

Fig. 7 is Kim Lam's Clock Card showing the hours she worked in a week in September. Although she has more than two and a half hours showing for the time she was in the store, only two hours overtime have been paid, as the extra minutes did not add up to 15 minutes per hour which was the agreed rate she would get for overtime. As you can see, there are no deductions. Although Kim came late on Monday and Thursday, she was only a few minutes late and deductions are only made after fifteen minutes late-coming.

Notice too that the final amount of £94.26 is *gross pay* i.e. without any deductions for income tax (called PAYE in the UK), or National Insurance Contributions, money paid to the government for welfare services such as hospitals, dental services, and supplemented medicines, and pensions when workers retire (see fig. 8).

Salaries – pay slips

We usually use the term **salaries** for monthly pay, and **wages** for weekly pay, but nowadays both are used to mean monthly, or weekly pay.

In fig. 8 there is an example of the weekly wage slip Kim Lam receives. As wage slips are produced to fit a company's requirements there are many different types, but of course there are similarities in telling the employee how much they have earned, and how much has been taken off in deductions. Kim's wage slip will tell her the following:

1 **Gross pay**, this figure is the total pay she has earned from the beginning of the tax year, which in the UK begins in April.
2 **Gross taxable**, you will see that all the pay she has earned is taxable.
3 **Tax**, tells Kim how much tax she has paid to the present date.

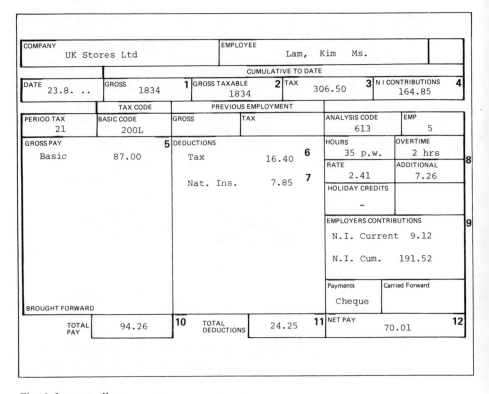

COMPANY			EMPLOYEE			
UK Stores Ltd			Lam, Kim Ms.			
			CUMULATIVE TO DATE			
DATE 23.8. ..	GROSS 1834	**1** GROSS TAXABLE 1834	**2** TAX 306.50		**3** N I CONTRIBUTIONS 164.85	**4**
	TAX CODE	PREVIOUS EMPLOYMENT				
PERIOD TAX 21	BASIC CODE 200L	GROSS	TAX	ANALYSIS CODE 613	EMP 5	
GROSS PAY Basic 87.00		**5** DEDUCTIONS Tax 16.40 **6** Nat. Ins. 7.85 **7**		HOURS 35 p.w.	OVERTIME 2 hrs	**8**
				RATE 2.41	ADDITIONAL 7.26	
				HOLIDAY CREDITS –		
				EMPLOYERS CONTRIBUTIONS N.I. Current 9.12 N.I. Cum. 191.52		**9**
				Payments Cheque	Carried Forward	
BROUGHT FORWARD						
TOTAL PAY 94.26		**10** TOTAL DEDUCTIONS 24.25		**11** NET PAY 70.01		**12**

Fig. 8 A wage slip

4 **National Insurance (NI) contributions** show the total amount she has paid from her salary, up to the present, in payments for her government pension, welfare services such as hospital treatment, dental treatment, and medical care. Although these are free in the UK, there are extra charges that have to be paid for medicines and dental treatment when the service is used.

5 **Basic pay** is the money she has earned during the week without any overtime, and you can check this with her clock card.

6 **Deductions** include tax, or PAYE (Pay As You Earn), which is calculated on two tables, Table A, which shows the **free pay** that is not taxed, and Table B, which shows **taxable pay**, which in this case came to £16.40.

In calculating tax there are two important items which are shown on the wage slip – **period tax** and **basic code**.

Period tax shows which tax week is to be worked out, and in this case it is week '21', which is 21 weeks from the beginning of April, the start of the new tax year.

The **basic code** is the code number given to an employee and worked out on the 'allowances' the government makes for employees. These 'allowances' concern whether the employee is married, has children, has to pay fees for courses, has any dependants who they have to take care of, like a sick parent, or other payments which the government will allow as being free from tax.

The **analysis code** and **employee** number, 613 and 5, are simply the company's code for their employees.

7 **National Insurance** is the weekly N.I. contribution that has to be made, and this too, like tax, is worked out on a schedule. In Kim's case, as she is a single person, the Table is Table A.

8 Kim's hours, overtime, and rate per hour are calculated to give her additional pay, and from her clock card we saw she worked two extra hours in week 21.

9 **Employer's contributions**, are the National Insurance (NI) payments employers have to make for their staff. And from the wage slip we can see that for this particular week £9.12 had to be paid, and so far Kim's employers have paid £191.52 in their contributions. But notice this is not deducted from Kim's wages.

10 **Total pay** for Kim was £87.00, plus £7.26 for overtime, making a **gross** total of £94.26.

11 **Total deductions**, her tax, £16.40, and National Insurance, £7.85 came to £24.25, which is taken off her gross pay.

12 **Net pay** came to £70.01 which would be her gross pay, less tax and insurance.

Exercise 12

Fig. 9 is Kim's contract of employment. From the letter confirming her appointment, on fig. 6, fill in the details listed below giving very general information.

Date the contract from the time she began her employment writing in Kim and her employer's names and addresses.

1 Write her **job title**.

2 **Remuneration.** Give her salary for the year.

3 **Hours of work.** What will her official weekly hours be, and which days will she work from and to?

4 **Holidays and holiday pay.** Explain how many weeks holiday she will be allowed after one year, and confirm she will get public holidays.

5 **Sickness or injury.** How many days a year will she be allowed if she is ill?

6 **Pension.** There is no need to give details, just confirm that the company has a non-contributory pension scheme.

7 **Disciplinary rules and disciplinary and grievance procedure.** This part explains what happens if a member of staff breaks the rules of the company either by constantly coming late, stealing, not working satisfactorily, or creating difficulties that interfere with the running of the business.

For this answer, all you need to do is mention that these points are covered by Rules 1 – 20 in the UK Stores Ltd. booklet on *Staff Employment and Conditions of Work.*

8 **Notice.** This tells Kim that if the firm wants to dismiss her, or she wants to leave, there has to be a period of time, usually one month, between the time notification of leaving is given and the time the employee leaves. UK Stores gives and expects one month's notice covering staff leaving.

PARTICULARS OF TERMS OF EMPLOYMENT

Given pursuant to the Employment Protection (Consolidation) Act 1978, s.1.

DATE..........................19....

TO: (Name and address of employee) ....

....

FROM: (Name and address of employer) ....

....

Delete words in one or other set of square brackets. Insert date only if previous employment counts as continuous with this employment.

Your employment began on .... 19.........

[No] Employment with a previous employer counts as part of your period of continuous employment with us [which accordingly began on ....19........]

The following particulars of the terms of your employment applied on........................

.... 19 ....:—

1. Job Title

2. Remuneration

Details must include scale or rate, or method of calculation, and intervals at which remuneration paid

3. Hours of Work

Details must include any terms or conditions relating to normal working hours

4. Holidays and Holiday Pay

Details must include entitlement to public holidays and particulars for calculation of accrued holiday pay on termination of employment

[P.T.O.

oyez The Solicitors' Law Stationery Society plc, Oyez House, 237 Long Lane, London SE1 4PU   F2829   3/83

Form C.E.1B   ★ ★

Fig. 9 A contract of employment

5. Sickness or Injury

*Details must include
statutory sick pay
as applicable and
any contractual
provision for
sick pay*

6. Pension

*Does not apply if
the pension scheme
is established under
Act of Parliament
and the employer
has to furnish details*

*Delete one alternative.

A contracting-out certificate issued by the Occupational Pensions Board is/is not* in force for this employment.

**7. Disciplinary
Rules and
Disciplinary
and
Grievance
Procedure**

*Does not apply to
matters relating to
health and safety
at work.
A person to whom
the employee can
apply in
(i) disciplinary and
(ii) grievance cases
must be specified*

8. Notice

*If the contract is
for a fixed term,
the date of expiry
must be given*

(A) By the employee

(B) By the employer

*The employee may
be asked to acknow-
ledge receipt on a
copy, but this is not
a statutory require-
ment.*

Received a statement of which the foregoing is a copy

Dated .... 19 .   ...

The structure of a company

2.1 An explanation of company structures, and personnel

There are two main types of companies, (a) those offering **goods**, such as machines, clothes, furniture and cars, and (b) companies which offer **services**, like banks, insurance firms, travel agencies and lawyers.

Whether the concern offers goods or services, if it is small, it will expect its employees to do a number of different jobs. A Company Secretary, who usually deals with the legal problems of accounting, in a small factory or advertising agency might have to deal with accounts, wages, contracts, employment of staff, as well as buying equipment and organising offices. A receptionist in a small fashion firm, could be expected to handle her own duties as well as the post, typing letters and sometimes modelling clothes for buyers.

In large organisations, who can offer both goods and services, departments are specialised and deal with only one area of work.

The sales department could be completely separate from the buying division.

The wages department could be separate from the accounts department which could be divided into purchases, sales, credit control, finance and internal auditing (internal checking) sections.

A very large company can be divided into four general areas:

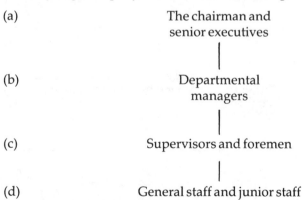

(a)   The chairman and senior executives

(b)   Departmental managers

(c)   Supervisors and foremen

(d)   General staff and junior staff

(a) The **senior executives** are the group of directors known as the **Board of Directors**, or just the **Board**. They are elected by the people who own a share in the company – the shareholders. The Board themselves will elect a **Chairman**, who is the chief executive of the company and has overall control of it.

At meetings – Board Meetings – the Chairman's influence is the most important as he has been elected because of his experience and knowledge of the markets the company is working in. The Chairman and Directors run the overall policy of the organisation planning its future, deciding on its products and services, and where, when, and how the company will develop.

On the Board there will be people with majority shareholdings in the organisation, a few people with important connections or titles to increase the firm's reputation, and specialists to advise the Board on technical or financial matters.

The **Chief Accountant** who controls the finances and investments of the organisation will probably be a member of the Board, and the **Company Secretary**, who is qualified as a lawyer and accountant might also be a member of the Board.

The Board will also select a **Managing Director**, who, as the title suggests, is a director involved with the total managing of the company from the factory floor up to the Board Room.

Some companies have senior management staff as directors, or junior or associate directors on the Board, and like the Chief Accountant and Company Secretary, they advise the Board on the advantages and disadvantages of policies that are being discussed.

(b) **Departmental managers** run the sections they are in charge of. The **Sales Manager** will organise all areas of selling in a company, linking with representatives and agents, and marketing and advertising who research to promote the company's products. The **Chief Buyer** will be responsible for getting the raw materials – the basic materials – used in production and manufacturing, and must know the cheapest and best products to use, where to get them, and how to use them so that quality and economy are maintained.

A **Production Manager** would be in charge of overall production, working with the **Chief Designer** and **Engineer** to make sure production is practical, economical, and efficient.

There are, of course, managers in the despatch, transport, and shipping departments who are responsible for packing and sending goods to customers, as well as handling all the documents needed for transporting consignments.

The **Chief Cashier** who runs the accounting side of the company would control bought and sales ledgers (accounting books recording sales and purchases), as well as credit control (keeping check of how much credit the company allows), auditing (checking the accounts) and preparing the final accounts for the Chief Accountant, who, as we have seen, is responsible for the financial side of the company.

There are also managers in personnel, who handle staff matters, warehousing, dealing with stocks and supplies, stationery and equipment, which supply offices, and general office managers who control the overall administration of offices.

(c) **Supervisors and foremen** are much closer to the hour by hour running of offices and sections in a factory.

Directors are responsible for the general policy of the company, the managers for making sure that policy is carried out, and supervisors and foremen in seeing that the details are handled directly by the staff who work under them.

In a typing pool, for example, the supervisor not only makes sure that everyone completes a reasonable amount of work every day, but that the work produced is correct in its form, layout, spelling, and wording. On the shop floor in a factory, the foreman will check to see that the products are produced in a given amount of time and reach the standards set by the management so that customers will not have to complain about bad workmanship or faults.

(d) **General staff and juniors** are the **secretaries** and **clerks**, in the offices, and the **machine operators** and **maintenance** people who handle the production and efficiency of the factories.

Secretaries usually work for directors or managerial staff and deal with personal correspondence, appointments, meetings, and travel arrangements. Clerical staff handle the 'paperwork' of the company, writing up accounts or feeding information into computers about accounts, asking for money the company is owed, or paying money the company owes, dealing with questions and problems concerning accounts, production, transport, shipping, with goods either being sent or received by the organisation, and on the production side of the company, actually building or manufacturing the company's products.

As we look at these areas of general administration and clerical work in later units, you will see what the day to day duties of the general staff and juniors are.

2.2 Departments and their functions

Fig. 10 is a diagram of the structure of a large company. All the departments will be linked with one another. Personnel, for example, will have dealt with every employee in the company. The **sales department** will deal with **accounts** – for customer accounts – the **legal department** – for sales contracts – **purchasing** – to find out what materials are being bought for the company's products – **production, design,** and **engineering** – to inform them what sort of goods customers want – and how successful, or unsuccessful sales of particular goods have been based on information they have got from **market research**. In addition, the **sales department** must work with **transport and shipping** making sure that orders have been completed and go out on time. They will also be involved with **stationery and supplies** for their own office equipment and materials, and **reprographic printing** to make brochures, catalogues, and price lists, as well as duplicating material used for their general administration.

Sales will also be in contact with **credit control**, who will tell them which customers can be given credit when they buy from the company, and **internal audit** who will make monthly checks of their office for accounts, equipment, and expenses. Like every other department, sales will be paid by the **wages section**, who will handle the salaries of their staff, the expenses of their representatives, who have travelling expenses, and the commissions of their overseas agents.

All departments will use **clerical staff** to handle correspondence,

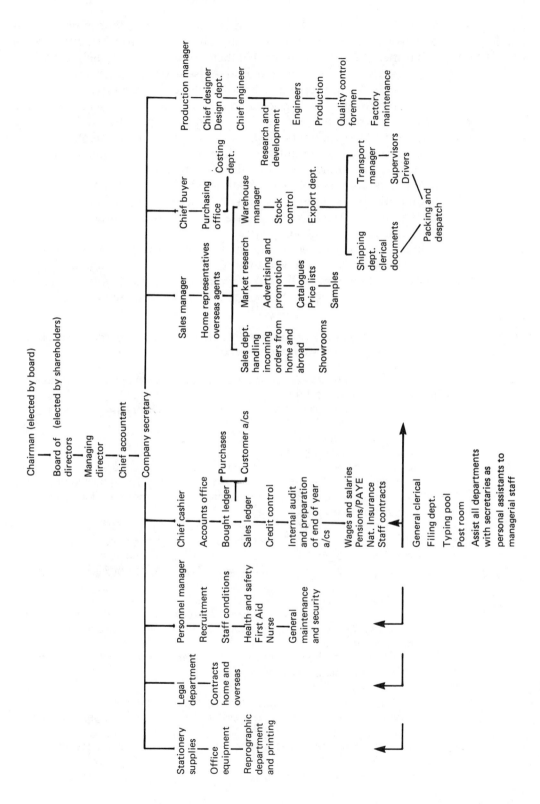

Fig. 10 The structure of a company

accounting, taking 'phone messages, filing documents, post, photocopying, and ordering supplies. The clerical staff may be moved from department to department to give them experience, or to help out when it is necessary. As we saw in the advertisement Kim Lam answered, the applicant had to be prepared to help out wherever necessary.

The **typing pool** will also handle work from all departments typing general correspondence, orders, invoices, packing lists, shipping documents, the contracts prepared by the legal department, accounting information, memorandums, which give the staff information about the company, and reports for various departments.

The **post room** will handle all internal and external mail for the organisation distributing letters, circulars, and accounts to their departments as the correspondence comes in and is sorted, or preparing post which is to be sent out.

In fig. 10, you can see that **general clerical, filing**, the **typing pool**, and **post room** are not just linked to other departments now and again, as the sales department might be, but are in constant contact with them, so their work is essential in keeping the organisation running smoothly.

Exercise 13

Use the correct **present simple** or **present continuous** tenses in the following conversation between two friends in an office.

Example: 'You (work) here?'
'Yes, I usually (work) in accounts, but I (work) in sales at present.'

Answer: 'Do you **work** here?'
'Yes, I usually **work** in accounts, but **I'm working** in sales at present.'

'What do you do here?'
'I (work)[1] in the sales department.'
'But this (be)[2] the accounts department, what (do)[3] here now?'
'I (help)[4] them for this morning. I always (move)[5] from department to department! Whenever someone (be)[6] away, they constantly (ask)[7] me to fill in for them!'
'You (sound)[8] like you don't (like)[9] it.'
'Oh, I suppose I (not mind)[10], I just (grumble)[11]. But if I (do)[12] a job I feel I must (do)[13] it well, and you sometimes (not do)[14] that if you (move)[15] from place to place all the time. And some sections (start)[16] at different times. So sometimes I must (get)[17] here at 08.30, and if I (work)[18] for Transport or Packing, I have to (arrive)[19] at 07.30.'
'(Pay)[20] overtime for that?'
'Oh, yes, if I (come)[21] early, they (give)[22] me overtime, but not at the time and a half rate, so I've made an appointment to see my supervisor about that.'
'When (plan to see)[23] him?'
'It (be)[24] a woman, and I (see)[25] her at 09.00 tomorrow in her office, and I definitely (ask)[26] for a higher rate of overtime.'
'Do you think you will get it?'
'I don't see why not, I believe other staff (get)[27] it now, and I know I work as hard as them, and if I understand the system, juniors (earn)[28] the same as senior clerks.'
'Well, good luck, I hope you get the rise. Will you be back in accounts tomorrow?'
'No, after seeing the supervisor, I (work)[29] in the wages department.'

Exercise 14   The list on your right is the name of a department, on the left, the matters the departments would deal with. Match the figures and letters together, e.g. 1 (c).

(a) Internal mail	1 Legal Department ☐
(b) An account your company must pay	2 Export Sales Department ☐
(c) A fault in one of your products	3 Wages & Salaries ☐
(d) A leak in the hot water pipe system	4 Transport ☐
(e) A sales contract for supplies	5 Post Room ☐
(f) The purchase of two new word processors	6 Reprographic Dept. ☐
(g) A mistake in your pay slip	7 Security ☐
(h) The demonstration of one of your company's machines	8 Bought Ledger ☐
(i) 200 photocopies of a sales letter to your customers	9 Quality Control ☐
(j) An overseas enquiry for one of your products	10 Advertising ☐
(k) An enquiry referring to a past order from purchases	11 General Maintenance ☐
(l) A minor accident in the machine shop	12 Office Equipment ☐
(m) A home customer's complaint about a delivery delay	13 Showrooms ☐
(n) A lock broken by force	14 Factory Maintenance ☐
(o) Booking space in an exhibition where your company's products will be shown	15 First Aid ☐
(p) A broken machine in the factory	16 Filing Dept. ☐

Exercise 15   **Verbs and nouns**

Verbs, words which explain **actions**, like walk, run, sit, talk, can be changed into **nouns**, words which explain **things**, e.g. to walk (verb), a walk (noun). Verbs sometimes have to become **noun forms** which we call **gerunds**, which are formed by adding **ing** to the verb, e.g. **walk** becomes **walking**. After you have selected the correct verb from the list below, use it in a gerund form.

Example: I talked about . . . the company
          to leave to stay to go.
Answer: I talked about leaving the company.

Sales managers organise all areas . . . [1] and are involved in . . . [2] and . . . [3]. Buyers, on the other hand, are responsible for . . . [4] the raw materials used in . . . [5].

Despatch, transport and shipping departments are responsible for . . . [6] and . . . [7] goods, as well as . . . [8] all the documents needed for . . . [9] consignments.

The Chief Cashier concentrates on . . . ,[10] the accounts side of the company. In his job you would have to enjoy . . . [11] with figures, and not mind . . . [12] late if you have not finished . . . [13] up the accounts at the end of the financial year. However, if you disliked . . . ,[14] . . . ,[15] or . . . [16] and . . . ,[17] you would avoid . . . [18] in accounts as you would think it was a waste of time . . . [19] all those figures, knowing that once you have finished . . .[20] the accounts at the end of the year, you would have to start all over again.

to do	to transport	to handle	to work out
to send	to manufacture	to advertise	to control
to write	to multiply	to market	to sell
to do	to get	to pack	to divide
to stay	to add	to deal	to subtract

Reception

The advertisement in fig. 11 has been put in the newspaper by a staff agency for a firm of lawyers. It comes from a Malaysian newspaper, but could be found in most situations vacant columns anywhere in the world.

RECEPTIONIST

A small firm of lawyers require a receptionist. The work will involve general reception duties and when necessary, help with typing, filing, operating a small switchboard, and making coffee for the senior partners.

Pay and conditions are excellent with a staff bonus and pension scheme.

If you are interested, phone Staff Finders Agency on (Kuala Lumpur) 72588 or 72615

Fig. 11 An advertisement for a receptionist

In a small company a receptionist might be expected to do a number of different jobs. In the above advert she will have to type, file – keep the records of the company in order – and handle a switchboard – taking calls and connecting them with the people who work in the different offices in the firm.

In larger organisations, where visitors are constantly calling, a receptionist may only be concerned with what the advert called 'general reception duties'. This work will include:

- Meeting all the callers that come into the company, and putting those with appointments in touch with the people they have come to see.
- Taking messages that are left by visitors, or by callers on the phone and making sure that the right message is delivered as soon as possible.
- Taking parcels, letters, or any other correspondence that is delivered 'by hand' and making sure it gets to the person it is meant for.
- Making a note of the callers who have visited the company, what their business was, when they arrived, and sometimes, when they left.
- Handling all the activities that relate to the reception area and this could include anything from flower arranging to selecting magazines or turning away an unwelcome visitor.

The receptionist is the first person visitors meet on the company's premises – their place of business – and the reception area is the first place they will see. The receptionist and where she works will be the first impression they get of the company.

If the reception area is untidy, the receptionist's desk full of reference books and bits of paper with messages, and the magazines the visitor is given are out of date, the caller will get the feeling that the company is untidy in its handling of business.

If the receptionist continues working while the visitor has to wait for her attention, then s/he will feel s/he is not important to the company, and this could be very serious if the visitor is a customer or client.

If the receptionist is not able to find the internal phone number of the visitor's contact in the firm, or does not know which floor or office the contact occupies, the caller will get the impression that the company is generally disorganised.

If the caller is left waiting for a long time after the receptionist has made her first call to the contact, and she ignores the visitor, or does not try a second call, then the visitor will become impatient or irritable – not a good start for the meeting s/he is going to go to.

It needs very little attention to avoid these problems. The reception area should be tidy, and information should be up to date – whether it is extension numbers, for an internal phone, or reference books, such as city guides and directories, or just magazines that are left for visitors to look at while they are waiting.

An acknowledgement of the visitor can be made by immediately saying 'Good morning/afternoon, can I help you?'

If you are on the 'phone you cay say to the person you are talking to 'Just a moment, please' then to the visitor, 'I'll be with you in a second' then you can finish your conversation, making it as brief as possible.

If you are filing or typing, then stop, the caller's business is more important at this moment.

We all feel nervous or strange when we go into a place that is new to us. Therefore, it is very important that a receptionist makes callers feel at ease – relaxed – when they first come into the company's building.

Many companies either have their receptionist's names on the desk in front of them, or their receptionists wear a 'name tag' as people always feel easier when they know the name of the person they are talking to.

The receptionist, in turn, should ask the caller's name, then repeat it back, so she will remember it.

Here is a situation in a Hong Kong company. Notice the way the receptionist deals with it.

RECEPTIONIST: 'Good morning, can I help you?'
VISITOR: 'Good morning, I've come to see Mr. Kwok Tai Lee.'
RECEPTIONIST: 'Mr. Kwok Tai Lee . . . and your name is?'
VISITOR: 'Miss Yeun Mei Tam.'
RECEPTIONIST: (Recording the name in the registration book) 'Miss Yeun Mei Tam . . . to see Mr. Kwok Tai Lee . . . do you have an appointment?'
VISITOR: 'Er . . . no, but I represent KM Computers and I believe Mr. Lee

deals with office equipment in this company.' (She hands over a business card).

RECEPTIONIST: (Takes the card, ready to file it with the other business cards) 'I think Mr. Lee only sees representatives by appointment.'

VISITOR: 'We phoned him some time ago, and he told us he is interested in some of our products.'

RECEPTIONIST: (Not sure whether Mr. Lee had been phoned, or if he is interested in KM's products). 'I can phone his office and see if he is in. Could you just tell me exactly what he was interested in?'

VISITOR: 'Most of our products.'

RECEPTIONIST: 'Would you like to sit over there while I phone through?' (She phones Mr. Lee's office, but does not mention the name of the person who answers the phone). 'Reception here. There is a Miss Tam to see Mr. Lee. She represents KM Computers and says her company contacted Mr. Lee some time ago and he told them he might be interested in their products, but she does not have an appointment. Is he in at the moment?' (She is told Mr. Lee is busy and cannot see anyone). 'Miss Tam I'm sorry, but Mr. Lee and his secretary are not available today. It would be better if you made an appointment at some time so you could be sure of seeing him.'

VISITOR: 'Is there anyone else I could see?'

RECEPTIONIST: 'It's very difficult to see anyone here without an appointment. But thank you for calling.'

Exercise 16

Answer the questions based on the above conversation:
1   How did the receptionist greet the caller?
2   Did she make any note of the call?
3   What did she say to confirm whether Miss Tam was or was not expected by Mr. Lee?
4   What was the receptionist going to do with the business card she received?
5   The receptionist was not sure whether Mr. Lee would see Miss Tam, even without an appointment. What did she say so she would not make a definite statement?
6   How did the receptionist announce who was calling Mr. Lee's office?
7   The receptionist did not say Mr. Lee or his secretary were not in, so what did she tell Miss Tam to say they could not be seen?
8   What expression did she use to suggest Mr. Lee preferred people to make an appointment?
9   How did the receptionist remember Miss Tam's name?
10 What did the receptionist ask to find out the particular products Miss Tam was selling?

3.2 Types of callers

From the above conversation, you can see that a company may have expected or unexpected callers. These can be divided into three groups:

Callers with appointments:
   Clients, customers, salespeople, demonstrators, company advisors such as accountants, lawyers, and officials.
Regular callers:
   Delivery people who bring goods, the post, messages etc., cleaners,

maintenance, and service engineers.

Callers without appointments:

Salespeople – representatives like Miss Tam. Casual enquiries from people asking about vacancies or trying to make an appointment to offer a service. Callers with complaints which can include anything from a complaint about a car parked in front of their office to a complaint about the company's products.

All callers are important to the company, whether they are overseas buyers or individuals complaining about the company's advertising. It is the receptionist's job to listen to them carefully, then, if they have an appointment, get in touch with their contact in the building. If a caller is delivering something, the receptionist should register the delivery, check the package or letter, and possibly sign a delivery book to say that the company has accepted it. Even if they are complaining about the wrapping paper the company's products are sold in, the receptionist should make a note of it, then pass the complaint on to the department dealing with that problem.

3.3 Registering callers

Callers with appointments can often have their appointments checked in an **appointments book** which gives the name of the caller, sometimes his/her company, their contact, and the date and time of the appointment:

CALLER	TO SEE	DATE	TIME
T Reiger L·S.M Ltd	B. Urs. Accnts	6·5. ——	10·30
E. F. Daws	Mr Colt Personnel	6·5.——	11·15
B. Adler Rhodes Ltd	F. Rass	6·5. ——	23·30

Fig. 12 An appointment book

Once the receptionist has confirmed the appointment and contacted the person the visitor is to see, on the internal phone, she could then say:

'Mr. Colt/Mrs. Vance, Mr. Colt's secretary/or Someone will be down in a moment to take you to his office.'
'Would you like to sit down for a moment, someone will be down/along to see you.'

Regular callers may have **business cards** with their own names and their company's printed on them. These can be fixed into a book, or onto a card in a small index box file under the **company's name**, as company names change less than the people they employ. Filing these cards will give you a permanent record of the company's name, address, and phone number.

Here is the card Miss Tam gave the receptionist during their conversation.

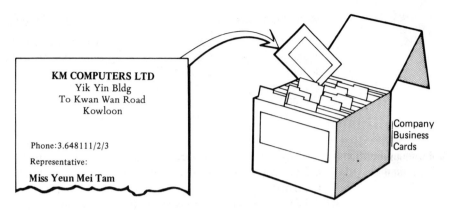

Fig. 13 Business cards

If the caller does not have a business card, they should still be recorded in a **visitors' register** giving details of their name, firm, reason for visit, or who they are seeing, date, and time.

NAME	FIRM OR ADDRESS	TIME	PURPOSE OF VISIT	SEEN BY	DATE 19......
D. Alexandre	J. J. T Ltd.	09.30	Meeting T.Drew	T.Drew	June 4
Miss Yeun Mei Tam	HK Computers	10.45	Comp. Sales Rep for Mr Lee	No appointment	June 4
R. Wong	584 Li Chit St H.K.	11.28	Maintenance/Carrier	P. NG.	June 4
P.N. Greenly	ABC Elec.	12.31	Conference	Mrs Devin	June 4
Mrs Senger	Acan Ce	14.25	Parcel Del. for Mr Kwok	Receptionist	June 4

Fig. 14 The visitors' register

Regular callers should be registered, even if the receptionist knows them very well, and they should produce some identity which shows they represent a firm.

No one should be allowed through reception into the main building unless accompanied by an employee of the company, or have had their identification confirmed by someone in the company and will be expected at a particular place, say, an office, or department. If there is a problem that the receptionist cannot handle, then security should be called to deal with it.

Exercise 17

Vocabulary
With some words we can use **un**, **in**, or **dis** to make their opposites. For example, co-operative – **un**co-operative; efficient – **in**efficient; agreement – **dis**agreement.

Make the opposites of the following words using un, in, or dis:

employment	controlled	like (meaning not to like something)	
usual	real	like (meaning not the same)	
secure	organised	active	successful
expensive	pack	expected	impressed
similar	prove	invited	associate
dependent	direct	connected	helpful

3.4 Communications – the phone

A large part of a receptionist's work will be in using the 'phone either delivering or taking messages, and of course this is true for all departments in an office.

When *delivering* a message on the 'phone make sure of what has to be said, and who the message should be given to. Writing the message down is very important. Write the message in note form, then read it back to the person giving you the information.

When you dial, make sure you have the right number as it is easy to turn numbers round, e.g. 661354, can easily be dialled 661345. Also make sure you have the correct **area code** as most areas have their own codes before the local phone number. The **area code** may be something like 01- or 1896- with the local number following, e.g. 01-548 9010, or 1896-558214.

Once you have got through, in a large company, there may be two delays before you can reach the person you want to speak to. The first delay could be the **switchboard** who will have to connect you to the extension number you ask for, that is the office phone number in the building.

The second delay could be because your contact's secretary answers the extension, or someone near has answered.

There is no need to give the message until you have reached either the person it is intended for, or someone who can pass it on to them.

Until you reach that person, all you need to do is tell them the name of your company, your name, and the extension number or the person you want to speak to:

YOU: (Dial the number; have the message you are going to deliver in front of you with a pen or pencil and paper as you may have to take some notes yourself).

SWITCHBOARD: 'Litton and Donald'

YOU: 'Stylon Ltd. here. Can I speak to Mr. Wilson on extension 621, please?' (or if there is no extension number) 'Can I speak to Mr. Raymond Wilson in the Sales Department. My name is David Lyne.'

SWITCHBOARD: 'Putting you through' (or) 'It's ringing for you.'

YOU: (The phone is answered) 'Stylon Ltd, David Lyne speaking. I've a message for Mr. Raymond Wilson from Alan Jones of our buying department.'

MR WILSON: 'Raymond Wilson speaking.'

YOU: 'Mr. Jones asked me to tell you . . . .'

If someone else answers, they may tell you they are going to get Mr. Wilson, or they may say he is not available, then you would tell them the name of your company, who you are and who the message is from, then ask if someone can take the message.

Once you have given them the information and they have read it back to you, get the person's name:

YOU: 'Could you read the message back to me, please? . . . Thank you, and could I just have your name, please?' (or) . . . Thank you very much, and your name is . . . (or) . . . Thank you, who am I speaking to?'

Exercise 18

Read the following message, which you have to give to Mrs. Rene Blake of Ardington's Stationery Co. on 01-772 9010 Extension 470.

Your office manager, Mr. Bruce Coleman wants to change his order (number B115) dated 5th March, from 500 A4 copy paper, to 1000 A4 copy paper, and the 5 packets of C5 envelopes should be changed to 5 packets of C3 envelopes. Could Mrs. Blake also cancel the 20 Group 4 ribbons that were ordered as we will not be able to use them on the new models of typewriters coming in? Delivery of the whole order, before the end of the week is still urgent.

If there are any problems could Mrs. Blake either contact Mr. Coleman on Extension 771, or his secretary on Extension 778?

1   Did Mr. Coleman order more or less copy paper?
2   Why did he cancel the typewriter ribbons?
3   What is Mr. Coleman's extension number 778, 771, or 470?
4   Is the message urgent?
5   Which department do you think Mrs. Blake works in?
6   Did Mr. Coleman change the type of paper he ordered?
7   When was the order placed?

Receiving a message

When you answer the phone, give the name of your company, or if you are on an extension, the extension number, and once the caller has been put through, the name of your department and your name, then ask who the caller wants to speak to.

Most companies have message pads like the one illustrated and information should be noted on them when possible.

Get the caller's name, his/her company's name and address, 'phone and extension numbers, and ask if they are going to call back.

YOU: 'Accounts department, extension 615, (your name) speaking.'

CALLER: 'Could I speak to Mr. Obi please?'

YOU: 'I'm afraid he's not here at the moment.'

CALLER: 'Could you take a message for me?'

YOU: 'Yes, I can do that.' (Using a message pad, if there is one, or a *large* sheet of paper) 'Your name is . . . (repeat) Mr. Jomo Kerede, and your company is (repeat) Nigerian Enterprises, and the address (repeat) Idewon Street, Ijebu-Ode, Ogun State, and the phone number, so Mr. Kerede can contact you, is . . . (repeat) 68151 . . . thank you, I've got that. What is the message?'

(Take the message carefully, then read it back to the caller, checking spellings when necessary, and using objects if the caller's pronunciation is not clear, e.g. Idewon Street, that is I for *Ink*, D for *Duck*, E for *Elephant*, W for *Window*, O for *Orange*, and N for *Nothing*, Idewon). Although there is a set alphabet for spellings, not everyone would be familiar with it, so common names are usually easier for you and the caller to use.

YOU: 'Are you going to call back, Mr. Kerede?'

CALLER: 'I might try tomorrow morning.'

YOU: 'I'll make a note of that, and I'll leave this message on Mr. Obi's desk now.'

CALLER: 'Thank you, goodbye.'

Messages

To: ....Dept: ....   From: ....

       Phone: ....

Date: ....   Address: ....

Time Rec: ....

Received by ....

Signed ....

Exercise 19

Fill in the above message form with the following information:

Mr. Takeo Iwanami, of the Nihon Bank, Nihon Building, Princess Street, London EC1, 'phone: 01-636 7419, cannot meet your Company Secretary, Mr. Paul Price, at 14.00 on Thursday March 15th, as he has been called away on urgent business. He expects to return on March 20th and should be free on the following Wednesday or Thursday in the afternoon. Could Mr. Price or his secretary phone to make an appointment for one of those days?

Use your name and decide what time you received the message.

One of your colleagues, in the sales office where you work, Narendra Patel, cannot come into work today as he has a very bad cold. He wants you to pass the message on to the sales manager Mr. Robert Wiseman and wonders if anyone could phone Harringtons, the company he was dealing with yesterday, and give them the information from the catalogue on his desk, page 44. There is a note of who they should speak to and details of Harringtons' address and phone number.

If there is a problem, phone Mr. Patel at home, his number is 761845. Make up your own date and time of the message, then fill in the message pad note, similar to the one in the illustration.

Exercise 20   Put the correct past simple or continuous tenses in the conversation.

Example: 'You (take) the phone message from ICM yesterday?'
            'Yes, but while I (take) it, John (interrupt) me.'
Answer: '**Did** you **take** the phone message from ICM yesterday?'
            'Yes, but while I **was taking** it, John **interrupted** me.

JAN: 'What (happen)[1] yesterday?'

ROMI: 'You mean why I (see)[2] the manager yesterday morning?'

JAN: 'Yes. I (hear)[3] it (be)[4] about a message.'

ROMI: 'It (be)[5]. I (take)[6] a phone message for him, but I (not get)[7] it right.'

JAN: 'Why? You always (take)[8] messages when you (be)[9] on reception in your other firm, and there (be)[10] no complaints.'

ROMI: 'I know. But yesterday, while I (take)[11] the information, some people (type)[12], and other (use)[13] calculating machines, and a few people (talk)[14], so I (not hear)[15] everything the person (say)[16] to me. Not only that, but while I (write)[17] Mary (interrupt)[18] me and asked me about a parcel I (deliver)[19] later. So I (not get)[20] the person's name right on the phone, nor the flight he (come)[21] into London on, or the hotel he (stay)[22] at, and I (not sign)[23] the message.'

JAN: 'And you (not say)[24] which Mr. Smith the message (be)[25] for. There are three of them in this company!'

ROMI: 'Who (tell)[26] you about all this?'

JAN: 'It doesn't matter.'

JAN: 'I'd rather you (tell)[27] me. If someone (say)[28] something about you, I (tell)[29] you.'

JAN: '(tell)[30] me, if they (tell)[31] you not to?'

ROMI: 'Perhaps not, but I wish I (know)[32] who it (be)[33].'

JAN: 'It doesn't matter. It's time we (leave)[34] now, anyway.'

ROMI: 'I know who (tell)[35] you! It (be)[36] Mr. Smith!'

JAN: 'Ah, but *which* Mr. Smith?'

UNIT 4

Filing

4.1 Organisation of a filing system

All companies and government departments will keep records in the form of files, because files are the memory of an organisation.

They are kept for **reference**, so staff can go back and find a design, a name, a deal, or an agreement that was made in the past. And they are kept as proof of what was written, in correspondence, bought or sold, in accounts, or agreed to, in contracts, or even said, in the minutes (the written records) of meetings.

Files could be arranged **alphabetically**, from A – Z, like your dictionary, which is really a 'file of words and explanations', or kept **numerically**, under numbers. Some files are even **coded**, kept under a combination of letters and numbers.

If a filing system is to work properly it will be:

Logical, and follow a pattern so that whether it uses letters or numbers a person will be able to go to any section of it and know how it works.

Comprehensive which means it will include all the information that the particular file covers. If any information is missing, the person searching will be able to know where it is, either because there is a note telling them that part has been taken out, or there will be a note explaining where else they can look for that information – this is called a **cross-reference**.

In your dictionary you might see a cross-reference under the word **enquiry** which will say 'look under I', as enquiry can be spelt **inquiry**.

Accessible which means the file can easily be reached by anyone who needs it. Some files are secret, and they may need special permission to search them.

Adaptable which means the file can be 'changed'. It may be made larger to take more information, or smaller, when old information is moved to another section.

Most files give **current** information, that is recent information and material that is not often needed, as it is out of date, is moved to a 'dead file'. However, there is usually a cross-reference for old information if you need it.

Convenient – the file should not be overloaded with too many papers so that it becomes impossible to handle it. Removing dead information is one way of keeping a file under control. Keeping it neat and tidy is another way of making it manageable. Using equipment like microfilm and computers is another way of getting the information faster, and reducing the amount of space taken up by filing equipment.

In summary, therefore, a filing system should be logical, comprehensive, accessible, adaptable, and convenient.

4.2 Methods of reference

We have seen that files can be classified (a) alphabetically, (b) numerically, (c) coded, under letters and numbers, or (d) chronologically, under dates.

Alphabetical classification

By using the alphabet we can use people or companies' names, addresses, for countries, districts, cities or towns. We can also file under subjects, which is a system many libraries use as a general heading for books, e.g. History, Accounts, Commerce, Economics, Mathematics, etc.

The rules for using the alphabetical method are:

Family names come first and other names follow:

> John Smith becomes Smith, John
> Alan Dell becomes Dell, Alan

As letters in the family name change, so they follow in sequence in the filing system:

> Aaron, Aasheim, Abraham, Agbulla, Akahito, Ashanti . . .
> (Notice that **Aar** is followed by **Aas**)

If there are common family names, like Smith, then the first name will decide the position in the file:

> Smith, Jack   Smith, James   Smith, Jane
> Smith, John

With two family names such as Au Yeung (a Chinese name) Smythe-Jones (an English name), Von Thadden (German), Van Gelden (Dutch), take the first part of the name for your filing position, e.g.:

Au Yeung, Wang Hing	Smythe-Jones, Christopher	Van Gelden, Dirk
Avon, David	Soames, Wilson	Vernes, Jules
Awami, John	Stafford, Grace	Von Thadden, Eric

Some companies have their owner's names, e.g. Roy Jackson (Repairs) Ltd. These are filed under the family name first in the usual way – Jackson, Roy (Repairs) Ltd.

If the company has two names – Dickens & Jones Ltd., or Marks & Spencer, the first family name will decide the position of the file in your system.

M', Mc, and Mac which often begin Scottish and Irish names should be filed under **Mac**, e.g. M'Farelane, McKinnley, MacDougal would be filed:

> MacDougal,   Jerry
> M'Farelane,   Mary
> McKinnley,   Joyce Helen

St before a name, which is an abbreviation for **Saint**, should be filed under **Saint**, e.g.

Saab,	Mikal
Sahil,	Sonny
St John,	Ian
Sato,	Keiko

Nothing comes before something is a rule in filing which means that names without initials come before names with initials, so Davenport, Paul: Drew, Eleanor; Davis'; Davis, Robert; will be filed:

Davis'	
Davenport,	Paul
Davis,	Robert
Drew,	Elenor

Initials by themselves come before names, so IMF; Ivanov, Nekita; Ibrahim, Mohammed; Imhof, Gerd; will be filed:

IMF	
Ibrahim,	Mohammed
Imhof,	Gerd
Ivanov,	Nekita

Geographical locations

Countries, districts or cities and towns can also be used with alphabetical filing where the 'places' are listed in alphabetical order, and under each 'place' the names of the companies or people are sub-listed, again in alphabetical order. Many mail-order companies who have agents selling goods through catalogues to local people list in this way, here is an example from the UK:

O

Orpington
  Bates & Co Ltd.
  Carter PLC
  Wade & James

Overton
  Alliance Insurance Ltd
  Errindale, D.
  Kelley & Benn PLC

Oxford
  AVR Ltd
  Acorn Electronics
  BTC
  Bains PLC

Subjects and miscellaneous

We saw that libraries often use a general title for subjects before putting books under authors' names or book titles. In an office when there is no need for individual lists of names, material may be filed under subject headings:

Personnel
  Absentees lists
  Applications (Jobs)
  Contracts
  Sick lists
  Staff Reports
  Vacations
Security
  Emergency Services
  Insurance
  Maintenance
  Work Rostas
Miscellaneous

At the end of the file there is a general file for various items under the title of **miscellaneous**. This file is for items which have no particular home in the files and may be odd records that are somehow linked to that section.

Numerical filing

Numbers, sometimes called **cyphers** are used by many organisations for their filing systems, as there is no limit to the numbers that can be used, or in combinations they can give more information than just a name.

A **filing index** might have all the numbers listed and from that the individual file can be pulled out and read.

Filing Index
860
861 ──────────────→
862
863
864

> **861**   Sato & Co Ltd.
> 1901 Nihonbashi 3-Chome,
> Chuo-ku, Tokyo 103
> Tel: 372-8133
> Stereo Equipment

Banks, insurance companies, and other institutions may also use a combination of numbers for information, the combinations below, for example, will tell an insurance company when the policy was taken out, the code of the policy (the type of policy it is – fire, accident, theft etc.,) and the number of the insured person:

Index

83	12	17	11875
84	1	17	11876
84	2	16	11877
84	2	17	11878

> 1984 – January – (17) Fire policy
> Client No. 11876
> Deravala, Jean (Miss)
> Greys Road, 42,
> Tunbridge Wells, Kent, TN1 1BX
> Phone: (0892) 66015

Figures and letters

The alphabet and numbers may be used with one another where letters could stand for a month, a year, or a grade, or a classification, and the figures a breakdown of the classification, or just a number on a list.

Dates

Sometimes items are filed by date in what we call 'chronological order', but a system like that could quickly get out of control if anything is misfiled and there is no index to locate it.

Exercise 21

Put the following names into their correct alphabetical order as you would if you were filing them:

Ruiz y Chanco, Maria	Arding & Hobbs Ltd.
Rolls Royce PLC	Marks & Spencer PLC
C & A Ltd.	McKinnley, J
Tesco	Masters, Helen
Cawley, David	MacAndrews, Ian
Tadokoro, A	Alliance Bank Ltd.
Chang, Lawrence	Evergreen Publications Ltd.
Reed, Stephen	Malaysian Exports
O'Malley, George	Kahn, Mohsin
Tsai, Yuan	Manning, Bernard
Peters, Liv	HMSO
The Institute of Bankers*	Zeidermann, J
Sarawak Shipping Co.	P & O Lines Ltd.
British Airways	Smith, James
Smith, Abel	St John, Brian
Sato, Keiko	Au Yeung, Wang Hing

*Note: The Institute of Bankers could go under 'T', for **The**, or 'I', for Institute, or 'B', as it is here and would be filed under 'Bankers' (The Institute of).

Exercise 22

Where do you think the items below the list of **subjects** would be found?

1. **STATIONERY**   2. **PURCHASES**   3. **ACCOUNTS**

4. **PERSONNEL**   5. **SALES**   6. **SECURITY**

7. **AGENTS**   8. **MISCELLANEOUS**

(a)   The address of one of your company's representatives
(b)   A list of people interviewed for a clerical job, last week
(c)   Details of a new alarm system
(d)   An order for 1 000 paper clips
(e)   A letter from a customer asking about your latest catalogues

(f)   A price list you received from one of your suppliers

(g)   A customer's letter asking for credit

(h)   A receipt for a bag the company bought someone as a leaving present

(i)   A list for year of people absent through illness

(j)   An order for 500 sheets of A4 paper

(k)   A record of commission paid to one of your representatives for the past six months

(l)   A copy of a brochure advertising electronic typewriters

(m)   A record of the rent your company has paid to its landlords for the past year

(n)   A bill for lighting and heating your company paid for the last quarter (three months)

Exercise 23

Section (A) are the names of countries, section (B), the names of cities your customers live in. File the cities under the correct countries

A

1 AMERICA   2 FRANCE   3 GERMANY   4 MALAYSIA   5 NIGERIA
6 SWITZERLAND   7 UNITED KINGDOM   8 MISCELLANEOUS

B

(a)	Lisbon	(b)	Kuala Lumpur	(c)	Manchester	(d)	Dallas
(e)	Lyon	(f)	Lagos	(g)	Bonn	(h)	Gothenburg
(i)	Ibadan	(j)	Bern	(k)	Le Havre	(l)	Leeds
(m)	Hamburg	(n)	Zürich	(o)	Chicago	(p)	Kano
(q)	Penang	(r)	Geneva	(s)	Boston	(t)	Tokyo
(u)	Kowloon	(v)	Glasgow	(w)	Frankfurt	(x)	Peking
(y)	Detroit	(z)	Paris				

Final note on file arrangements

We saw that with a name like 'The Institute of Bankers' files will disregard the article 'The' and 'Institute of' using 'B' as the indicator of where to find the file.

In filing we also tend to disregard (ignore) titles like Lord, Dr., President, etc., and use the family name of the person, e.g. Denning (Lord); Schweitzer, A (Dr.); Lincoln, Abraham (President). We also ignore **contractions**, e.g. M'Chester, and use the whole name for filing – **Man**chester. We disregard **articles** and **prepositions** such as 'The'; 'A'; &; of; for; by etc. Therefore, 'The Times' becomes Times, (The). Kingman of Singapore becomes Kingman, (Singapore of).

Names with numbers like 'The First National Bank of America' will probably be filed as America, (The First National Bank of) or possibly First National Bank, (of America).

There are no hard rules in filing other than the system must be understood by everyone using it, and must be **consistent**, so that if one method is used, then it must be carried through the whole organisation so everyone knows whether they should look under 'numbers', 'names', 'articles', or 'prepositions'. Some bookshops use authors' names to list their books, others, book titles, but none uses both methods at the same time.

4.3 Sorting

Large companies usually stamp documents with the word **File** to show they are to be put away as they are finished with. However, some documents may still be needed for a while and are noted and filed under **Pending,** generally loosely so they can be taken out when needed quickly.

When sorting documents make sure they should be filed, then if there are a lot of them, sort them into order. **A concertina file** (fig. 15), can be used for putting papers in alphabetical or even numerical order.

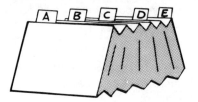

Fig. 15 A concertina file

While sorting you could need some basic equipment: **bulldog**, or **paper clips** to hold things together, fig. 16, or transparent sticky tape (Sellotape) or **ring tabs** to strengthen the material, fig. 17.

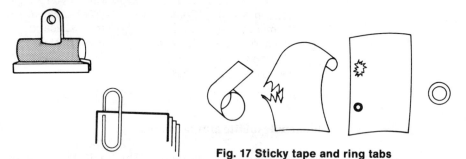

Fig. 17 Sticky tape and ring tabs

Fig. 16 Bulldog clip and paper clip

Filing tabs, or **tags**, will be needed to identify letters, numbers, or subjects, fig. 18, and **highlighters**, or coloured pencils to underline important points on the documents for reference, fig. 19.

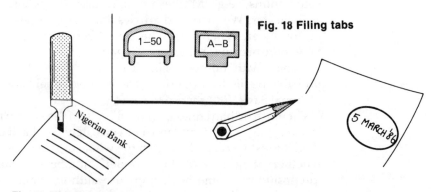

Fig. 18 Filing tabs

Fig. 19 Highlighters

A **punch**, and **stapler** are often useful, the punch for making holes in **ring files**, the stapler for clipping papers together, fig. 20.

Fig. 20 A punch, stapler and ring files

Guide rules for filing

- Do not file anything unless it has been passed for filing which usually means it has a stamp – **File** – on it.
- Remove 'dead files' to keep the paperwork under control. But always make sure that 'out of date' files can be put away. If in doubt, do *not* take out, *always* get permission before destroying or removing files.
- Record all files that have been temporarily taken out in a 'charge out' or 'absent' book. Note when the file was taken out and who took it, and put a note or marker indicating the file is missing.
- Never leave a file open on a desk, or just lying around. Files often have confidential (secret) information in them.
- If papers are no longer wanted, destroy them in a 'shredder', a machine which cuts unwanted papers into thin strips. If the company does not have a shredder, then tear the file or papers yourself.
- Keep filing cabinets locked and other systems secured.
- Make sure that whatever system of filing you use will be 'consistent' – a regular system that never changes – so everyone will know exactly how it works.

4.4 Filing equipment

There is a large selection of filing equipment which companies can buy, and their choice will depend on the cost and needs of the firm. Small companies will use inexpensive simple systems while larger organisations might need the more complex electronic systems.

Indexes

An **index** is a list of files in a system. An index may tell you where to look for a file, what is in the file, or give you a **cross-reference** if, for example, a name in the file has been changed, if a customer has moved, or the company has been taken over (bought) by another firm, e.g. TRM (Textiles) Ltd., look under 'The Logan Corporation PLC'.

The index could be kept in a **card-box file** like the one used by receptionists for a quick reference to a company's visitors, see fig. 13, p.33. The 'contents section' of this book is really a type of index telling you what each section contains.

Box files and ring files (binders)

Files could be kept in boxes with strong clips to hold the papers down, or in ring binders like the one illustrated in fig. 20. An alphabetical index separates the different sections. Many students use these for notes and handouts, with the indexes listing different subjects or parts of a subject, e.g. grammar – Tenses, Articles, Gerunds, Infinitives, Prepositions etc.

Visible card trays

Each tray has overlapping cards which are found by visible plastic strips giving you the name of the file you need as an index. Coloured signals mark particular divisions or cards that are needed. Although the system is quick to use, the information is limited so that they are mainly used for addresses, price lists, stock records, or quick references.

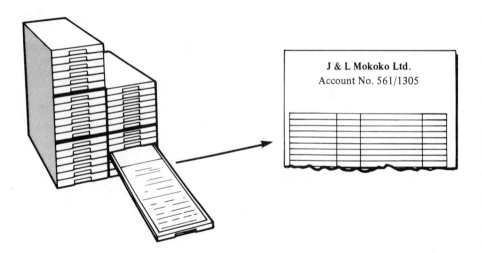

J & L Mokoko Ltd.
Account No. 561/1305

Fig. 21 A visible card system

Vertical filing cabinet

In these metal cabinets files are usually suspended (hung) on metal rails with their titles in plastic tabs at the top of the cardboard files.

Although the cabinets are fireproof and secure because they can be locked, and the files last for a long time, the system takes up a lot of room in an office (fig. 22).

Lateral filing cabinets

Files are placed beside each other, laterally, with their titles showing vertically, up and down. The system can be stacked up, built one on top of another, but lateral files are not as easy to use as vertical ones and are not as secure, as the files are exposed open (fig. 23).

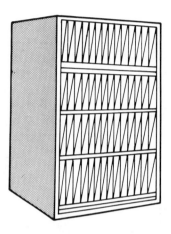

Fig. 22 Vertical filing cabinets

Fig. 23 A lateral filing cabinet

Microfilming

This method uses photographs of material on (a) rolls of film, like those in a camera; (b) in jackets, holding up to 60 frames; (c) punched cards, with one frame; (d) microfiche, single sheets of film holding from 98 to 420 A4 documents.

The files are seen through a **viewer** which, in some systems, can reproduce a copy of the document (fig. 24).

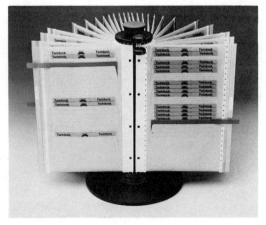

Fig. 24 A microfiche reader and printer (left) and storage equipment (right)

The system is fast to use, saves space, and documents are protected. But as the system is expensive for both equipment and processing films only large organisations use it.

Computer filing systems

Microprocessors – electronic typewriters with computing facilities – can be used for filing material. Microfilm can be used with the microprocessor's screen for viewing. Information can also be stored on **magnetic tapes** (similar to the one in a cassette), or **floppy discs** both of which will reproduce information on the microprocessor's screen (fig. 25).

Digital optical recorders are also being introduced, where information is recorded on a disc and a laser beam picks it up then reproduces it on a VDU (Visual Display Unit) screen.

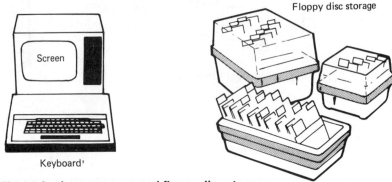

Fig. 25 A microprocessor and floppy disc storage

Desk racks and mobile trolleys

For larger sized information storing such as computer print outs, there are desk racks and trolleys which can be moved about, fig. 26.

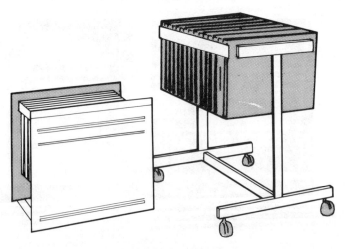

Fig. 26 A desk rack and mobile trolley

Exercise 24   Choose the right answer from the three alternatives:

1   If you want to make holes in paper for ring binder filing would you use a   (a) stapler   (b) paperclip   (c) punch?

2   A document that needs a temporary file would be put in a   (a) folder   (b) pending file   (c) dead file

3   VDU stands for   (a) Various Documents Used   (b) Visual Documents Unit   (c) Visual Display Unit.

4   Lateral means   (a) across   (b) up and down   (c) in and out.

5   A micro-processor is   (a) an electric typewriter   (b) an electronic typewriter with computer facilities.

6   If you came across a name like The 17th Century Antiques Shop, would you look under   (a) 'T'   (b) 'A'   (c) 'S'?

7   Shredders are used for   (a) destroying unwanted files   (b) filing unwanted files   (c) holding files together.

8   A floppy disc is   (a) a roll of film   (b) a single sheet of film holding a number of frames on it   (c) a way of recording information for a micro-processor.

Exercise 25   Put the correct tenses in the brackets

Example: 'You (finish) filing yet?'
'Yes, I (finish) an hour ago but I (sort) through correspondence since then and I'm not finished with that.

Answer: '**Have** you **finished** filing yet?'
'Yes, I finished an hour ago but I**'ve been sorting** through correspondence since then, and I'm not finished with that yet.'

AMY: 'You (finish)[1] with the JMS file yet, Peter? You (use)[2] it all morning.'

PETER: 'I (deal)[3] with that one and all the others on my desk. I (put)[4] documents and correspondence in alphabetical order, and I just (reach)[5] 'J', so I (not finish)[6] with it yet. Why do you want it?'

AMY: 'The manager (ask)[7] me to get it for him, a few minutes ago. How long will you be?'

PETER: 'Well, I (work)[8] on the others for two hours, and (arrange)[9] the 'Js' since 10.00, but I suppose you can have it, if you sign it out, use the charge out book.'

AMY: 'I suppose you'll be pleased when we get this microfiche system in. You ever (work)[10] with microfilm before?'

PETER: 'I (use)[11] a microprocessor, when I (be)[12] in my last company, but I never (file)[13] using microfiche, but I (hear)[14] they are not difficult to use. If they (had)[15] one here this morning, it (be)[16] much quicker, and your manager (find)[17] what he wanted faster.' (third conditional).

AMY: (Taking the file) 'Thanks anyway. I'll bring it back when I (finish)[18] with it.'

PETER: 'You (check)[19] that all the papers are in it?'

AMY: 'Yes, I (checked)[20] that. I don't think I (forget)[21] anything.'

PETER: 'You (forget)[22] something.'

AMY: 'What's that?'

PETER: 'You (forget)[23] to sign the charge out book!'

Exercise 26   When you have finished exercise 25, answer these questions based on it.

1   What has Peter been doing all morning?

2   How far has he got in his work?

3   What filing system is the company going to get?

4   What filing system did Peter use in his last firm?

5   Does Peter think the microfiche system is difficult to use?

6   What did Peter ask Amy to check before she left?

7   Why did Peter call Amy back?

8   Who was Amy getting the file for?

Buying and selling

Companies buy and sell goods and services. Goods are the raw materials they use in manufacturing their own products, and services are the skills and help they get from professions such as lawyers and advertising agencies, and from their own staff whose experience, knowledge, and services they hire.

All these goods and services go into producing the company's own products or services which they sell on the market.

Firms find out about what they can buy from agencies in their own country and overseas, trade organisations, advertising, and material sent to them in the form of catalogues (which give illustrations, descriptions and price lists of goods), brochures (a smaller, but more expensive catalogue), booklets (small books advertising products), leaflets and pamphlets (single sheets of paper for one particular thing the company is selling).

Here is an item from a catalogue for a micro-photographic filer:

- *Micro-filer AB-20*   Works on cartridges that make 4000 A4 prints on plain paper. Does not need toner or maintenance other than a six-monthly check.
- Lenses allow reproduction from fiche or roll film and produce clear images on its screen.
- Size: 405 x 405 x 50 mm.
- Price: $2000.00 plus 10% tax.
- Guarantee: 2 years for service and parts.

Exercise 27

Refer to the catalogue description above and answer these questions:
1 Does the machine need maintenance?
2 What system will it record information on?
3 How much does the machine cost?
4 Does it need special photocopying paper?
5 How would you inspect documents filed with this system?

Percentages

In the catalogue description of the micro-photographic filer, it said the price was $2 000.00 plus 10% tax, so the total price, the **gross** price (i.e. the **net** price plus additions) would be $2 200.00.

Per cent means **per hundred**. To find out what percentage a number is of another, e.g. 60 of 500, we take 60 as a fraction of 500 which is $^{60}/_{500} \times 100\%$ which is $^{60}/_{500} \times ^{100}/_{1}$ which is $^{6000}/_{500}$ or $6000 \div 500 = 12.00$ or 12%

If we already know the percentage, we might want to know what it is in other terms. For example, a company might increase its prices by 11% for items costing $300. How much would that be in money terms?

Divide 300 by 100 to find 1% or $300/100 = 3.0$, then multiply by 11, that is $3.0 \times 11.00 = \$33.00$

Exercise 28

Calculate the first number as a percentage of the second, then choose your answer from the alternatives:

1 $48 as a percentage of $680.00   (a) 14.16%   (b) 18.02%   (c) 21.4%
2 75 kg as a percentage of 225 kg   (a) 35%   (b) 33.33%   (c) 45.0%
3 25c as a percentage of $1.50   (a) 16.66%   (b) 19.25%   (c) 21.00%

Change the percentages into other units:

4 12% of 400 kg   (a) 48 kg   (b) 59 kg   (c) 65 kg
5 15% of $250.00   (a) $31.00   (c) $35.00   (d) $20.00
6 10% of $2000.00   (a) $300.00   (b) $350.00   (c) $200.00

5.2 Phone enquiries and terms of sales

A company may not have any information about a supplier's goods or services and you could be asked to phone them for details. In this case the guide below would help you:

- Have some writing material ready to take down the information
- Make short notes of exactly what you want to ask for and who you need to contact – you might be given a name, a title, like the works supervisor, an extension number, or a department
- Explain which company you are phoning for, and who you are – 'My name is . . .' 'I work in the Buying Department . . .' 'I'm phoning for Mr . . . our buying manager'
- Explain what you want:
  'We are interested in . . .' 'I'm phoning about the advertisement you placed in the July issue of (name of magazine)'
  'I wonder if you can give me information about . . .'
- Give any information you think will help the supplier:
  'The (product) will be used for . . .' 'We are really interested in the (product) as we need it for . . .'
- Explain whether you will take an alternative, as this saves time:
  'If style X isn't available, then Y or Z will do'
  'The colour doesn't matter'/'We are only interested in black'
  'Have you anything less expensive.'/'We might go a few dollars more if the quality was better'
  'Could you offer us something else?'
- Explain if you want any special terms:
  (a) **Discount**
      'Do you offer a **cash discount**[1], if we pay in seven days?'
      'Would you offer a **quantity discount**[2] if we doubled the order?'
      'What sort of **trade discount**[3] does your company offer on these products?
      [1]**Cash discounts** are offered for quick payment, usually within a week.

[2]**Quantity discounts** might be given if your company buys a large 'quantity' of the product.

[3]**Trade discounts** are allowed if companies are in the same 'trade', e.g. a publisher and bookseller; a cloth manufacturer and tailor; a wood warehouse and a carpenter.

(b) **Payment**

'How do you want us to pay for this?'

'Where do we send the cheque?'

'What method of payment would you prefer?'

(c) **Delivery**

'Could you deliver within the next ten days?'

'How long would you need for delivery?'

'Should we send someone round to pick it up, or can you deliver it?'

(d) **Confirmation**

'Would you send us written confirmation of the price? Send it to (name, department, and address).'

'Can Mr . . . phone you back to confirm the price?'

'I'll pass this information on to my manager/supervisor and h/she'll be calling you soon.'

- Make sure that the person you have spoken to can be contacted direct once you have the information. So take their name, department, and extension number if you do not have it.

Exercise 29

Example: 'I'd . . . Mr. Day in your accounts department, please.'
         'Mr. Day isn't here at present, could someone else help you?'
Answer: 'I'd **like to speak to** Mr. Day in your accounts department, please.'

Your company is D & G Traders Ltd., 35 South Street, Liverpool DS1 RP2. Your stores manager has asked you to contact the sales department of United Shelving Ltd. to ask if they could send you 40 of their 'Litewate shelves' Catalogue No. LS 357, sizes 250 x 40 x 5 cm, if they are not available, then from the same catalogue number he will take 300 x 45 x 5 cm, but nothing else, as the shelves are to be used for filing purposes.

Delivery must be within 10 days, and if that cannot be arranged then someone will pick them up. Payment will be by cheque, as you have an account with United Shelving, and should come to £160.00 gross, less 10% trade discount, so the **net** amount should be £144.00. Your official order will follow as soon as United confirm by post or telex that the shelves can be supplied.

Read the conversation through once, then supply your part in it.

YOU: 'Can I . . .[1] in your Sales Department who can help me with an order?'

MR. DAY: 'Bob Day, Sales Manager here, can I help you?'

YOU: 'Yes, I am phoning for Mr . . .[2] our . . .[3] He would like to know if . . .[4] 40 of your . . .[5] sizes 250 x 40 x 5 cm?'

MR. DAY: 'Oh, I know Mr. Jackson, your Stores Manager, will you hold on a moment, I check if we have them in stock. (Pause) I've checked the stock-list on the VDU, but I'm afraid we don't have the size you want.'

YOU: 'Do you have . . .[6]' (alternative)

MR. DAY: 'One moment. Yes, the VDU shows we've got those'

YOU: 'Could you . . .[7]' (delivery)

MR. DAY: 'I'm sorry, but our transport is booked for the next fortnight.'
YOU: 'We can . . .[8]' (collect)
MR. DAY: 'That'd be okay. D'you know anything about paying for this?'
YOU: 'We'll . . .[9] (payment) . . .[10] (account)'
MR. DAY: 'And what about your order note?'
YOU: 'We'll . . .[11] as soon as we . . .[12] (confirmation)
MR. DAY: 'Okay, the price will be £160.00.'
YOU: 'That'd be the gross price. Mr. Jackson said that as we are in the trade, there'll be . . .[13] so the net price . . .[14]'
MR. DAY: 'Ah, yes. That's right. I'll get the confirmation off to you right away.'
YOU: 'Thank you. If there are any problems could you . . .[15] on extension No 7713.'

5.3 An order

Here is an example of the order that D & G Traders Ltd. would send once United Shelving confirmed they could supply the goods.

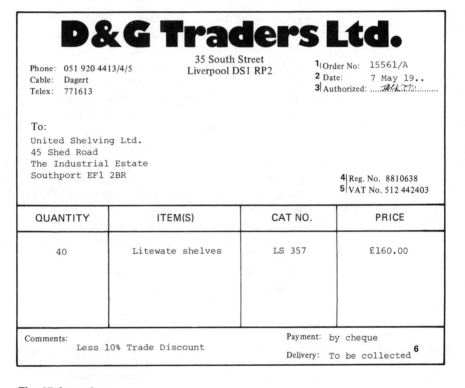

D&G Traders Ltd.

	35 South Street	
Phone: 051 920 4413/4/5	Liverpool DS1 RP2	[1] Order No: 15561/A
Cable: Dagert		[2] Date: 7 May 19..
Telex: 771613		[3] Authorized: ...*Jackson*...

To:
United Shelving Ltd.
45 Shed Road
The Industrial Estate
Southport EF1 2BR

[4] Reg. No. 8810638
[5] VAT No. 512 442403

QUANTITY	ITEM(S)	CAT NO.	PRICE
40	Litewate shelves	LS 357	£160.00

Comments:
    Less 10% Trade Discount

Payment: by cheque
Delivery: To be collected [6]

Fig. 27 An order

Notice in the order, fig. 27, there is a number recording the particular order, for references[1]. There is the date of the order[2], and its 'Authorisation', i.e. the person who made the order[3]. There is also the company's registration number[4], which is the number the company has registered itself under, and a VAT number[5], the purchase tax number, called a **value added tax** number which gives the tax on the value of the goods and is included in their price. There are also, under 'comments', discounts, payment methods and delivery terms[6].

5.4 Written enquiries

A guide for writing an enquiry will be similar to that of phoning for information as written and spoken English are very similar today:

- Explain what your company does, or who it is:
  We are a sports equipment manufacturers
  We are a large retail store
- It is sometimes useful to tell the company you are writing to how you heard about them:
  Our associates (do not use 'friends') J.F. Electronics advised us to write to you
  We are answering the advertisement you placed in the January edition of '(name of paper or magazine)'
  Your Consulate in our country advised us to contact you
- Say what you want, giving any information that might be helpful to the supplier
  We are interested in . . . These products will be used . . .
  We would like to know more about . . . which we are thinking about selling in our country
- If it is a particular product you want, tell the supplier if you will take an alternative in colour/size/style/price etc.
  If this is not available in red, then green, or blue would be acceptable
  If the item under Catalogue No. 671A is not in stock, then 580A or 981C would be considered.
  We might consider another quality if the price was right.
- In a first enquiry, discounts, prices, and delivery dates are not usually discussed, but it might be helpful to give some idea of what your company wants to pay, or when they want the goods delivered:
  We would not like to go above $. . .
  We cannot consider anything more than $. . .
  As the summer season is close, we would expect delivery in the next few weeks.
- You would close the letter by saying you hope to hear from the suppliers soon, or hope to receive the catalogue/brochure/samples/patterns in the near future.

Exercise 30

You work for 'International Fashions PLC', Regent House, Regent Street, London W1A 1AA, and your sales manager David Walton has asked you to write to 'Denby Manufacturing', 500 Li Chit Street, Wanchai, Hong Kong, asking them to send you their latest catalogue of summer dresses.

You want a price list which includes c.i.f. charges to London (that is the cost, insurance, and freight charges to London which will be included in their prices), and you would like to know what trade discount they are offering and when they could deliver once they have received the order, as you are writing this letter on the 10th February 19 . . and your company is preparing for the summer season.

Fill in the spaces in the letter below with the information you need.

Universal Computers PLC

Chairman:
C. Dukes ACCA

Directors:
E.F.Aldern FCA
R.T.Canley FIC

Regent House
Regent Street
London W1A 1AA

Phone: 837 7182
Cable: Interfa
Telex: 889163

. . . . 1A

Sales Manager, 1B
. . . .
. . . .
. . . .
. . . .

Reg. London 661451
VAT No. 341 7901 32

Dear Sir,

I am writing to you on behalf of ..., 1C our ..., 2 who would like
your ...3 which we want to add to our range which will appear in
our ...4 next ....5.

Could you also send us a ...6 giving ...7 London prices. We
would also like to know ...8 you could offer us, and ...9 as we are
...10.

We would appreciate an ...11 reply as the matter is ...12.
Thank you

Yours ...13

. . . . 14
Peter How

Exercise 31

Your company is Singapore Office Supplies Ltd., 1003 Sims Avenue, Singapore 1438, and you have been asked to fill out the Order Form below which is going to The Sharn Furniture Co., 198-D Princep St. Singapore 7.

You want six 'Siteasy Executive Chairs', Catalogue No. 461D at $300.00 each. Five 'Standard' typist chairs Cat. No. 3025/C 405 x 405 x 50 mm at $130.00 each. 1 Single Pedestal Desk Cat. No. 2150/M at $500.00.

Payment will be by cheque, and delivery within 14 days of them receiving the order, No. 8817CN. And there will be a 5% cash discount off the gross price.

The order has been authorised by Mr. R. Singh, the stores manager.

```
ORDER No. ..............    Singapore Office Supplies LTD
Date: 8th May 19..          1003, Sims Avenue
                            Singapore 1438

                                              Tel: 7472260



To:
.........................
.........................
.........................
.........................
```

QUANTITY	DESCRIPTION	CAT NO.	PRICE
			$ 1
			2
		Gross Price	
Payment:			3
Delivery:		Net Price	
Terms:			
Authorized:			

5.5 Advice notes and delivery notes

Advice notes are sent by suppliers to their customers to inform them that the goods they ordered have been sent on to them. The method the goods have been sent by is mentioned, e.g. air, sea, road, or rail, and often a description of the goods and packing is listed so the customer can recognise the parcel if it has to be collected from an airport, rail or truck depot or dock.

Delivery notes give information about the goods and method of transport. There are usually two copies, one which the customer keeps, the other which s/he signs to show that the goods have been delivered. However, if you sign a delivery note, and do not examine the goods, then make a small note by your signature saying 'goods not examined'; this is in case they are damaged inside the crates or boxes they are packed in.

Inside the boxes there will be a **packing list** explaining what the containers are holding.

```
DELIVERY NOTE 89103/15              The Sharn Furniture Co.
                                    198-D Princep Street
Date:  17 May 19..                  Singapore 7.
Customer Order No. 8817CN           Tel:  6998105
Customer:                           Telex:  916013
Singapore Office Supplies Ltd.
1003 Sims Avenue
Singapore 1438


  QUANTITY          GOODS                      NOTES


      6      Siteasy Exec Chairs  Cat. 461D    Carriage 'paid

      5      Standard Type Chairs  "   3025/C  for' - Company,

      1      Sgle Pedstl Desk      "   2150/M  G&C Haulage

                                               Grace Street

  Accepted by .............                    Singapore.

  For .....................
```

Fig. 28 A delivery note

The delivery note in fig. 28 refers to the order in Exercise 31. Notice there is no price listed, although in some cases the delivery note is a copy of the invoice, and prices would be listed. However, there is a comment that 'carriage' (transport) has been paid, and the name of the 'haulage company' (the trucking company) is mentioned. There is also a place for the signature of the person who accepts delivery, in the case of small parcels this could be a receptionist, and the name of the company they represent would also be written.

Some companies simply have a sheet as part of a **delivery book** which the driver will ask the person accepting the goods to sign. This book simply gives the name of the company receiving the goods and a brief description of the consignment, e.g. 'office furniture'; it also lists the other calls the delivery van is making that day or that week.

Exercise 32

Use the **simple past**, **past perfect**, or **past perfect continuous** in the following sentences:

Example: He came in. He shut the door. (After)

Answer: After he **had come** in, he **shut** the door.

1 She typed the letter. She put it in an envelope. (As soon as)
2 He got the file. He put the documents in it. (When)
3 He worked in the company for six years. They dismissed him. (After)
4 I lived in Kowloon. I moved to Hong Kong island. (Before)
5 She worked in Personnel for a long time. They transferred her tc Accounts. (Before)
6 I studied Chinese for ten years. I understood the language. (Before)
7 I posted the catalogue. I forgot to include the price list. (Although)
8 He left the office. The phone rang. (As soon as)
9 He worked on the report for three weeks. He realised he had received the wrong information. (When)

10   They thought about asking for a rise for a long time. They finally went to see the manager. (Before)

Exercise 33

Choose the correct answer from the three alternatives:
1   If you are in the same trade as your supplier, he will give you a   (a) cash discount   (b) trade discount   (c) quantity discount.
2   A single sheet of paper advertising a product is called a   (a) brochure   (b) leaflet   (c) catalogue.
3   The registered number of a company on its correspondence and documents is   (a) the number given to it when it registers as a company   (b) its registered tax number   (c) the number that should be quoted when you correspond with it.
4   The net price of a product you are buying is   (a) the total price without discount taken off   (b) the average price of the product   (c) the price with all discounts taken off.
5   90 kg as a percentage of 500 kg is   (a) 15%   (b) 16%   (c) 18%.
6   VAT means   (a) value and tax   (b) value added tax   (c) value after tax.
7   If a company offers you a 5% cash discount off an item costing $800, then you would pay   (a) $790   (b) $760   (c) $750.
8   Signed delivery notes show that   (a) goods have been sent   (b) goods are at a depot   (c) goods have been received.
9   A packing list explains   (a) who packed the parcel   (b) what the contents of a parcel are   (c) how the parcel is packed.
10   A 'haulage company' is a   (a) railway company   (b) an airline   (c) a trucking company.

5.6 Accounts documents

Invoices

The most important document in a sales transaction (deal), whether selling goods or services, is the **invoice**.

An **invoice** is simply a 'bill' giving the customer details of what they have bought, how much the items are, and the discounts allowed. In an overseas invoice for exports or imports there is also information about the **cost** of shipping, **insurance**, and **freight**, the actual charges made by the shipping company. Also we saw earlier that if the seller is taking care of these details, he will charge the customer for these arrangements quoting a 'cif' price, e.g. cif London, cost insurance freight charges to the port of London, or cif New York, charges to the port of New York.

Fig. 29 is an example of an invoice.

The invoice in fig. 29 shows[1] the invoice number, 6713/D, which is the exporter's reference, and the buyer's order number, 577B. The date, 9 June . . , is the date the invoice was prepared.

In[2] there is the seller's name and address, and[3] the buyer's name and address.

[4]Shows the seller's catalogue number, followed by what was bought.[5] '@' means 'at' this price, and in the last column[6] there is the final price, e.g. 500 @ $2 each = $1000 – this is called 'an extension'.

A 10% 'sales tax' has been added, which is like the value added tax (VAT) we saw used in the UK, so the figure at[8] gives us a **gross total** for sales.

```
┌─────────────────────────┬──────────────────────────────────────────┐
│ Invoice No:   6713/D    │ ¹ ELECTRO SUPPLIES                        │
│ Order No:     577B      │   (Hong Kong) Ltd.²                       │
│ Date:     9 June 19 ..  │   352 Westlands Road                      │
│                         │   Quarry Bay                              │
│                         │   Hong Kong                               │
│                                                                     │
│   International Importers Inc.                                      │
│   605 West 50th Street 3                                           │
│   New York 10020                                                   │
│   USA                                                              │
├──────────────────┬───────────────────────┬────────────────────────┤
│ Tel: 6—884115—3  │   Telex: 5528 EK       │   Cable: LECTRON       │
├──────────────────┴───────────────────────┴────────────────────────┤
```

Cat. No.[4]	Items [5]		Price US$
C451/N	500 VHS Video Tapes	@ $2.00 each	1000.00[6]
C511/N	1000 cassette "	@ $1.20 "	1200.00
E 61/0	5 VDUs (Standard)	@ $300.00"	1500.00
D 51/E	30 cass. records.	@ $40.00 "	1200.00
			————
			4900.00
		Add 10% tax	490.00[7]
			————
			5390.00[8]
		Less 20% Quantity Disc.	1078.00
			————
			4312.00
Add Dock Charges 50.00			
Insurance to			
New York 70.00 [9]			
Freight 165.00			285.00
		cif New York	4597.00[10]
			————
E & O E			

Fig. 29 An export invoice

However, a 20% **quantity discount** has been taken off, so the **net total** for sales is $4312.

The exporter has arranged for shipment and paid all the costs including insurance[9] and this came to $285 – the cost, insurance, and freight charges to New York. These are added to the net sales total giving a final 'cif New York' price of $4597[10].

A pro forma invoice is sometimes sent to a customer when they want to know what charges will be, or if they have to pay before getting the goods. The pro forma invoice will be an exact copy of the 'original invoice', except the words 'pro forma' will be typed or stamped on it.

Debit notes

Sometimes a customer is **undercharged**, because a mistake might have been made in a quotation. Or when the invoice was worked out a mistake was made in the calculations, e.g. 5 @ \$300 = \$1400, not \$1500. In this case a **debit note** is sent to the customer explaining the undercharge, fig. 30.

Debit note No. DN 671 Ref: Order No. 577B Date:　21 June 19 ..	**ELECTRO SUPPLIES** (Hong Kong) Ltd. 352 Westlands Road Quarry Bay Hong Kong

Dr. International Importers Inc.
605 West 50th Street
New York 10020
U.S.A.

Tel: 6–884115–3	Telex: 5528 EK	Cable: LECTRON

	Amount US\$
<u>Undercharge</u> on Invoice 6713/D 5 VDUs @ \$300.00 each \$1400.00, should be \$1500.00. We apologize for any inconvenience this may have caused.	<u>100.00</u>

Fig. 30 A debit note

Credit notes

Credit note No. CN 883 Ref: Order No. 577B Date:　29 June 19..	**ELECTRO SUPPLIES** (Hong Kong) Ltd. 352 Westlands Road Quarry Bay Hong Kong

Cr. International Importers Inc.
605 West 50th Street
New York 10020
U.S.A.

Tel: 6–884115–3	Telex: 5528 EK	Cable: LECTRON

	Amount US\$
<u>Returned</u> 5 VDU packing cases @ \$10.00 each	50.00

Fig. 31 A credit note

If the customer is **overcharged**, because a mistake was made in a calculation or s/he has returned a packing container which had been charged for, then a **credit note** is sent, explaining why the money has been credited to the customer's account.

Credit notes are also given when goods have been returned because they were not satisfactory, e.g. did not work, or were poor quality, or if they were the wrong goods, fig. 31.

Statements

Companies send their customers **statements of account** monthly or quarterly (every three months). The statement tells the buyer how much s/he owes from the previous month, if there is an 'outstanding balance' from last month; what they have bought during the period; how much they have paid; if there are any additions to their account, such as **debit notes**, or if any deductions have been made, **credit notes**.

30 June 19.. Customer a/c No. I/5316/US	**ELECTRO SUPPLIES** (Hong Kong) Ltd. 352 Westlands Road Quarry Bay Hong Kong	STATEMENT

International Importers Inc.
605 West 50th Street
New York 10020
U.S.A.

Tel: 6–884115–3	Telex: 5528 EK	Cable: LECTRON

Date	Items	Debit [1]	Credit [2]	Balance US$ [3]
June 1	Account Rendered [4]			580.00
" 5	Invoice No.6502/D	3162.75		
" 6	Cheque		580.00	3162.75
" 9	Invoice No.6713/D	4597.00		7759.75
" 14	D/N 668	50.00		7809.75
" 18	Cheque		7000.00	809.75
" 29	C/N 883		50.00	759.75
E & O E [5]				

Allow 2½% Cash Discount if paid within 14 days [6]

Fig. 32 A statement of account

[1]The **debit** side of the statement is the money the buyer owes. The **credit** side is the money s/he has paid[2]. The **balance**[3] is a running total adding and subtracting each item.

The statement in fig. 32 begins with an **account rendered**[4] which is the money that was owed from the end of last month, $580[5]. E & O E stands for **errors and omissions excepted**, which we also saw on the invoice. This means that if there has been a mistake, the seller has not charged for something, or has overcharged, or undercharged, s/he has the right to correct it. The debit note and credit note are ways the adjustment (the correction) can be made. [6]Finally, the seller on our statement will allow the buyer to deduct a 2½% **cash discount** if the statement is paid within two weeks.

5.7 Accounting systems

Bought and sales ledgers

There are manual, hand-written or typed, accounting systems and mechanised systems which are semi- or completely computerised. All systems work on the same principle of recording sales and purchases in a **day book** giving the total of the day's trading, and entering individual sales and payments into customers' own accounts from the invoices sent to them, and payments from cash or cheques received. Customers' personal accounts are kept in a **sales ledger**, which could be a book with a manual system, or a **ledger card** with a mechanised system. Purchases and payments are entered into individual suppliers' accounts in a **bought ledger**, which can also be a book or a ledger card.

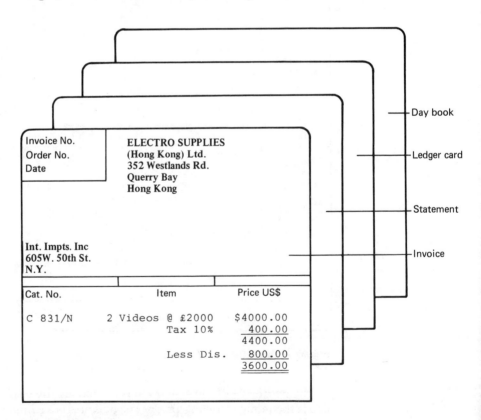

Fig. 33 Alignment system

Alignment systems

Most bookkeeping today uses a manual or mechanised system of alignment where with carbons one entry is recorded on an invoice, statement, ledger card, and day book, fig. 33.

On the same principle of 'carbon copies', several invoices can be duplicated if they are needed in different departments, once the top copy has been sent to the customer, e.g. Accounts, Sales, Filing, Transport – for a Delivery Note, Warehouse, and Stock Control.

Exercise 34

London Booksellers PLC LTD	STATEMENT OF ACCOUNT

55–59 Portman Way London WC1B 3HH

31 March 19..

Tel: 01 772 3331/2/3/4
Telex: 881503 London

To:

Atlantic Books Ltd.
Ighodaro Road
Jericho, Ibadan.

Reg: London 6190153
VAT: 43 7514 32

Date 19..	Items	Debit £	Credit £	Balance £
1 Jan	Account Rendered			350.00
8 "	Invoice 7156		258.00	608.00
11 "	Cheque		350.00	258.00
16 "	Debit Note DN 541	120.00		138.00
17 "	Invoice 7251	740.00		878.00
24 "	Credit Note CN 123		112.00	990.00
28 "	Cheque		400.00	490.00
O & E O				

Allow 3% Trade Discount if paid within 7 days

What are the seven mistakes in the above statement?

Exercise 35

If you send a debit note to a customer asking for extra payment you must send a letter with it explaining the reason for the undercharge and apologising for the inconvenience. With the information given, put in the addresses and find the missing words from the list.
Exporter: Mr. Takeo Yamada, Eikow Building, 25-28 Hongo, 1-chome, Bunkyo-ku, Tokyo 13, Japan.
Importer: D.S. Okoronkwo, 570 Ikorudu Road, Ilupeja, Lagos, Nigeria.
Debit Note No. D/N 891
Order No. 5516A

```
                                          15th May 19..


              1
       Dear Mr ..........,

                       2          3
       Please find ..... our ..... ..... No. D/N 891 for $200.00 which
              4        5                                  6
       is for an ..... on ..... No. 5712, your Order No ..... .
             7                                        8
       The ..... was because of a mistake made in an ..... where 30
                 9                           10          11
       units ..... $50.00 each should have read ..... not ....., the
                             12
       difference being ..... .
                           13            14        15
       We apologize for the ..... and will ..... your ..... next month.
                               16
       We hope this has not ..... you.

                     17
       Yours ........

                      18
       Takeo Yamada

       ..... .......
```

200.00   statement   debit   Sales Manager   extension   @
enclosed   error   1500   invoice   inconvenienced   undercharge
5516A   mistake   Debit Note   sincerely/faithfully (choose one)   1300.00

Exercise 36　　Choose one of the terms, of the three given in the conversation which concerns a customer, Mr. Bartlet, who is complaining to Miss Shaw in the accounts department of his supplier.

MISS SHAW: 'Hallo, Accounts here, can I[1] **help|assist|aid** you?'

MR. BARTLET: 'Yes, it's Bartlet and Company here. I'm[2] **telling|saying|enquiring** about the discount you allowed us on our last[3] **bill|invoice|credit note** for 10 dynamos which we bought from you.'

MISS SHAW: 'Could you give me the number, please?'

MR. BARTLET: 'It's 761/A, and my[4] **registered|VAT|account** number with you is 56-88143.'

MISS SHAW: 'I've got your[5] **credit|ledger|accounting** card now. I see we [6]**let|offered|allowed** 10 per cent[7] **quantity|cash|trade** discount, as you are in the same line as us.'

MR. BARTLET: 'But you have overcharged me.'

MISS SHAW: 'In that case we would send you a[8] **credit|debit|advice** note. But I can't see how we overcharged you from the copy invoice I have here.'

MR. BARTLET: 'The dynamos cost $250.00 each and there were 10 of them, so that [9]**does|makes|works** $2500.00, packing, delivery and insurance at $170.00, which makes a total of $2670.00, less 10% discount which is[10]**$277.00|$267.00|$287.00**, should make a final total of [11]**$2403.00|$2393.00|$2383.00**, but you've charged me $2420.00.'

MISS SHAW: 'I can see the problem. You are[12] **including|deducting|dividing** the delivery charges and insurance with the amount. Discount, however, is only calculated on the[13] **net|gross|final** total, which is $2500.00, so your discount should only be $250.00, not $267.00 which it would be on $2670.00. If you like I could send you a[14] **copy|pro forma|double** invoice, with a note to explain the calculations.'

MR. BARTLET: 'No thank you. I understand the situation now. You've been very helpful. Goodbye.'

MISS SHAW: 'Please call us if you have any problems in future, goodbye.'

UNIT 6

Banking

6.1 Banking services

There are four main clearing banks, also called commercial banks, in the United Kingdom – Barclays, Midland, National Westminster, and Lloyds, with a few other banks making up a group that offers services to commerce, industry, and the general public, similar to the services offered by banks everywhere in the world.

As well as investment services and advice, these banks offer:

(a) Current accounts
Paying in books
Cheque books
Cheque cards
Cash cards

(b) Deposit accounts
Paying in slips
Interest

(c) International payments
International Girobank transfers
Banker's cheques
Bills of exchange
Letters of credit

(d) Standing orders
Direct debits
Credit transfers
Credit cards
Overdrafts/loans
Bank statements

(a) Current account services

Current Accounts do not offer interest to depositors in the UK, although they do in many other countries. The bank holds the customer's money until it is needed.

Deposits are registered in a **paying in book** with the customer writing in all the cash and cheques s/he has received on a **paying in slip** and copying the details on a **counterfoil**. The paying in slip is stamped and kept by the bank, the counterfoil is left in the paying in book with the bank's official stamp confirming that the money has been paid in, fig. 34.

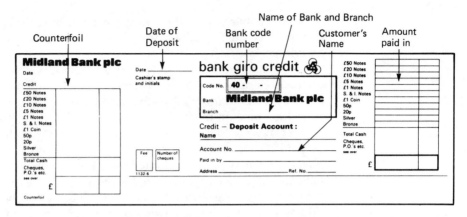

Fig. 34 A paying in slip (*Courtesy of Midland Bank plc*)

Deposits can be paid into any bank, and through the 'clearing system', which is used to balance money paid into banks and money paid out from them. The credit will go to the customer's account.

Cheques

A book of cheques is given to a customer with a current account. Some companies may have two or three different accounts with a bank to pay for different things, e.g. suppliers a/c no. 1; wages and salaries, a/c no. 2; rent, rates, heating etc., a/c no. 3.

Most cheques are 'crossed' with two parallel lines drawn or printed across them. This limits who they can be paid to, or gives time for the cheque to be 'cleared' through the bank clearing system, fig. 35.

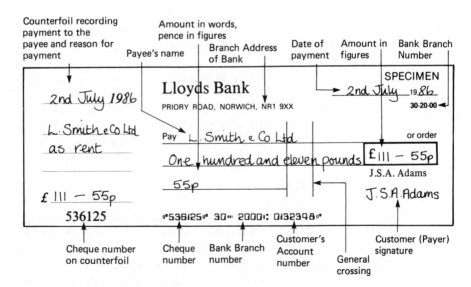

Fig. 35 A cheque with general crossing (*Courtesy of Lloyds Bank*)

The customer paying the cheque, the **payer**, records the payment to the person receiving the money, the **payee**, on a counterfoil, just as he does with a paying in book.

The cheque in fig. 35, is **generally crossed**, which means no particular instructions are given in the crossed lines on it. After the payee's name there are the words 'or order'. This means that the payee can **endorse** the cheque (sign his name on the back) and have it paid into anyone's account. So L. Smith can write 'pay B. Green' on the back and sign the cheque, and it will be paid into B. Green's account. If the bank knows the customer, or the payee, they may pay cash immediately for the cheque; if not, the payee will have to wait about three days for the cheque to be cleared.

Special crossings have the name of the bank the cheque should be paid into, which is usually the payee's account in his own branch, fig. 36.

Special crossing showing which bank the cheque should be paid into

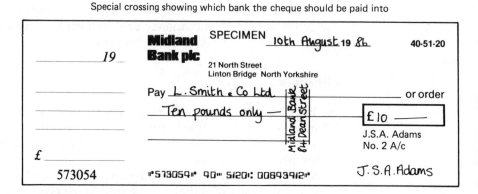

Fig. 36 A cheque with special crossing (*Courtesy of Midland Bank plc*)

A cheque with the words **account payee only** (a/c payee only) written in the crossing shows the payer wants to limit the cheque to only being paid into the payee's account.

Open cheques do not have any crossing and can be cashed by anyone who says they are the payee and presents them to the bank, although the bank will ask the payee to endorse (sign the back) of the cheque.

The most unsafe cheque is a **bearer cheque** which simply says 'the bearer' after the word 'pay'. Anyone can cash this cheque without an endorsement.

Mistakes

If you make a mistake in writing a cheque, put a wrong figure, or name, then you must cross out the mistake clearly, initial it, then write the correction.

If you have paid a cheque and want it stopped, then the bank will give you a special form to complete which asks for the details of the cheque, payer, payee, date, number etc. However, a bank will not usually stop a cheque on telephone instructions alone.

Cheque cards

To guarantee the payment of an amount, people paying by cheque usually have to produce a **cheque card**. Most cards have a limit of £50 on them, which is the amount the bank guarantees (promises) to pay the payee. However, larger amounts are accepted every day, but the payee generally has to wait three days before the cheque is cleared through the payer's account.

Cash cards

Banks and some other financial organisations like building societies now have **cash dispensers**, fig. 37, which allows customers to draw up to £100 in cash by putting a **cash card** into the machine and pressing their personal card code.

A magnetic tape on the card registers their Personal Identification Number, PIN number, which cannot be seen by anyone, and the money is produced.

The advantages of these cards are that they can be used outside of banking hours, and dispensers now give statements and balances on the customers' accounts.

Fig. 37 A cash dispenser (*Courtesy of Midland Bank plc*)

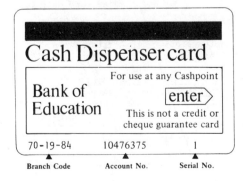

Fig. 38 A cash card (*Courtesy of Banking Information Service*)

(b) Deposit accounts

Banks have different savings accounts, but the most commonly used by the general public is the **deposit account** where customers deposit their money by using a paying in slip as they do with a current account. They then withdraw it using a withdrawal slip, which they get in the bank.

The advantage of a deposit account is that it gives the customer interest – extra money – for saving with the bank. The disadvantage is that although money can be deposited in any branch of the bank, it can only be taken out at the branch the account is held, and the bank can ask for notice, advanced warning, of about ten days before they pay out a large amount.

(c) International payments

There are different ways importers can pay exporters using bank services and these include (i) International Girobank transfers, (ii) banker's cheques, (iii) bills of exchange, and (iv) letters of credit.

(i) **International Girobank transfer** is simply a credit transfer from one person's account to another's. The payer simply makes out a Girobank transfer form, giving details of the payee's account, the amount to be paid etc., and the bank will debit the payer's account and transfer the money.

(ii) **Banker's cheques**, sometimes called **bank drafts** are actually cheques bought from a bank for the amount you want to pay the payee, plus bank charges, and the cheque can be sent to the person direct. Since the cheque is drawn on the bank's **own** account and not a private depositor's, there should be no problem for the payee in cashing it.

(iii) **Bills of exchange** are used all over the world to settle international payments. Most companies have their own bills of exchange printed for them, as there are no official forms.

An exporter (seller) writes out the bill of exchange, and he is called the **drawer**. He simply says that the importer (buyer) must pay a certain amount at a certain date. The importer is called the **drawee**.

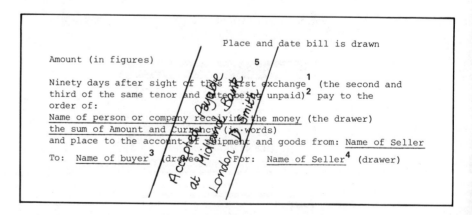

Fig. 39 A bill of exchange – term draft

If the importer, the drawee, must pay the bill immediately, the bill is called a **sight draft**, because it is paid when he 'sees' it. If he can pay it 30/60/90 days later, it is called a **term draft**.

With a **term draft** the drawee must sign across the face of the bill that s/he has 'accepted' it, i.e. he accepts the responsibility of paying it. The bank in the importer's country will usually hold the 'shipping documents' (the documents the importer needs to collect the goods) until the importer 'accepts' the bill, fig. 39.

1 **Tenor** of the bill – the time it is to be paid after presentation which in this case is 90 days.
2 The number of copies of the bill
3 The drawee's signature (buyer's signature)
4 The drawer's signature (seller's signature)
5 Acceptance of the bill and place it will be paid, in this case Midland Bank, London

(iv) **Letters of credit** are used when an importer (buyer) pays an exporter (seller) through a bank.

The importer fills out an application form asking his bank to pay the exporter. He gives information about the goods, when they will be shipped, how much he will pay, how long he wants the letter of credit to run, and who will be paid.

His bank will then pick an **agent bank** in the importer's country and tell them to pay the importer for them, once the shipping documents have been delivered by the exporter to them, the agent bank.

The importer hands the shipping documents over to the **agent bank** who pay him, then send them to the importer's bank who will transfer the money to the agent bank.

The importer, who has already had the payment taken out of his account, then collects the shipping documents so that he can get the goods.

(d) Standing orders

A company or person can pay a fixed amount of money every week, month, or quarter etc., through a bank by **standing order**. They make out a form instructing the bank to pay, for example, their landlord, rent on the 1st of every month, and the bank will transfer the money to the landlord's account.

Direct debits

With a standing order the amount is usually fixed, and the payer orders his bank to pay. With a **direct debit** the bank's customer tells the bank that his creditors (the people he must pay) can have money transferred from his account, to theirs when they present bills for payment. In this case, the payer will make very sure that they know their creditors very well. The advantage of the direct debit is that it saves time and money in paying bills, and the amounts can be changed when necessary, and in some cases,

Deposit Account
Application Form

To Anybank plc | Branch

I/We enclose £ | (personal cheques to be payable to Anybank plc)

Please open a Deposit Account in my/our name(s)

Surname	Mr/Mrs/Miss/Ms
Forename(s)	Date of Birth
Occupation/Employer	
Surname	Mr/Mrs/Miss/Ms
Forename(s)	Date of Birth
Occupation/Employer	

Address

Postcode | Telephone

Signed | Signed

Both to sign for Joint Accounts | Date

Standing Order for Regular Saving

To Anybank plc | Branch

Until further notice please transfer to my/our Deposit Account

Number

(Your branch will complete the number when opening your new account)

The sum of £ on day of each month

Starting | month | year

Please debit my/our
Current Account Number

Account Name(s)

Signed | Signed

Date

Fig. 40 An application: deposit account; standing order

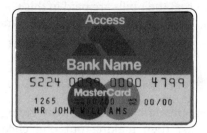

Fig. 41 A credit card (*Courtesy of Access*)

1. Place your card in the machine in the way shown above. This raises the screen, then

2. Key in your personal number.

3. Select the service you require.

4. If you require cash, enter the amount required on the keyboard.

5. Remove your card and the cash from the machine and await your receipt.

Fig. 42 Instructions on using a cash point

creditors might insist that their bills are paid in this way, particularly if their customer is buying goods from them on credit and paying at regular periods.

Credit transfers

A customer can pay many different creditors by giving the bank a list of the payments to be made, then making out one cheque to cover all the payments.

The money is then transferred to the different creditors' accounts, or can be paid to them 'over the counter' if special instructions are given. Many companies pay their employees' salaries in this way.

Credit cards

Customers with current accounts and good reputations are allowed to have **credit cards**.

By simply signing a 'sales voucher' which with the credit card registers what the customer has bought, a customer can be given credit in a shop, restaurant, or anywhere that will accept that particular credit card.

The amount of credit the customer can get will depend on their creditworthiness (how much credit the central credit card office will allow them). This can usually be checked by a 'phone call to the issuing office.

Customers are charged monthly interest on outstanding bills (amounts to be paid).

Some credit cards, such as Barclaycards, can also be used as cheque cards, and there are machines which will accept credit cards as cash cards.

Overdrafts and loans

Customers with current accounts are sometimes allowed overdrafts or loans.

An **overdraft** lets the customer draw more money than is in his or her account, up to a limit, say £100. So if the account only has £50 in it, the bank might allow the customer to draw up to £150 over a period of time.

A **loan** is a more formal agreement with the bank, and a contract saying the customer will repay the loan at a fixed rate of interest within a certain time is signed. The loan, say £500, is immediately put into the customer's account and interest is charged from that date. As with an overdraft, the bank will ask for some sort of security, perhaps shares, or a mortgage, or something the bank thinks it can sell if the customer does not repay the loan.

Bank statements

A bank will regularly send a customer a statement of their account telling them what payments have been made and what money has gone into the account.

A **credit** balance means there is still money in the account, a **debit** balance shows the customer has **overdrawn** the account, and this might soon be followed by a letter from the bank manager asking the customer to clear (pay) the outstanding balance (the amount s/he owes the bank).

If the customer does not clear the outstanding balance, then any further cheques the customer writes will 'bounce' that is they will not be paid by the bank. The cheque will be returned to the payee with a remark saying 'Refer to Drawer' – in other words, ask the drawer why the cheque has not been passed.

J.S.A. Adams [1]		Midland Bank plc 52 Oxford Street London W1A 1EG			
		Statement of Account			
198..	Sheet: 68 Account No. 21021850 [2]	DEBIT	CREDIT	BALANCE	
JUL 1	BALANCE BROUGHT FORWARD [3]			220.35C	
JUL 2	100072	111.55		108.80C	
JUL 11	100073 [4]	60.00		48.80C	
JUL 14	DIRECT DEBIT INSURANCE CO. LTD. [5]	10.00		38.80C	
JUL 18	A & C ELECTRONICS [6]		128.00	166.80C	
JUL 21	STANDING ORDER TV LICENCE [7]	20.50		146.30C	
JUL 23	BANK CHARGES [8]	11.20		135.10C	
JUL 25	100074	160.00		24.90D [9]	
JUL 28	ROYSTON SALES LTD.		290.00	265.10C	
JUL 30	100075	55.00		210.10C	
JUL 30	BALANCE CARRIED FORWARD [10]			210.10C	

Fig. 43 A bank statement

1 Bank customer's name
2 Customer's account number with the bank
3 Balance from the previous month
4 Cheque numbers
5 Direct debit payment to an insurance company
6 Money received from a customer
7 Standing order paid quarterly
8 Bank charges for bank's administration, or periodic interest on a loan or overdraft
9 Debit balance as customer has drawn out too much money
10 Balance which will be carried forward into August

Exercise 37   Mark whether the following statements are *true* or *false*

		True	False
1	Deposit accounts offer cheque book facilities	☐	☐
2	A cheque with a special crossing naming the branch of a bank, can still be cashed anywhere	☐	☐
3	Open cheques can be cashed by anyone	☐	☐
4	Some companies have more than one current account with a bank	☐	☐
5	A cheque card can be used in a cash dispenser	☐	☐
6	You can draw money from a deposit account at any branch of a bank	☐	☐
7	A banker's draft is a bank cheque	☐	☐
8	Some cash cards can be used as cheque cards	☐	☐
9	With a standing order, the payee can demand payment	☐	☐
10	With a credit transfer, the payer can pay many different creditors on one cheque	☐	☐
11	Deposit accounts offer overdraft facilities	☐	☐
12	Most banks will not ask for a security for a loan	☐	☐
13	A 'sight bill' allows you time to pay after it has been presented to you	☐	☐
14	Current accounts do not usually offer interest in the UK	☐	☐
15	A letter of credit gives the buyer time to pay	☐	☐
16	A counterfoil in a paying in book is used to record details of cash and cheques put into the bank	☐	☐
17	In a bill of exchange, the drawer is the person who will receive the money	☐	☐
18	To endorse a cheque is to write on the back of it	☐	☐
19	A 'bearer cheque' has no payee's name on it	☐	☐
20	A 'term draft' is a bill of exchange which will be paid after a period of time	☐	☐

Exercise 38   What five things are wrong with the cheque below? It is a specially crossed cheque for £530.63 and is from T. Matheen who is paying A.C. Holdings Ltd. direct into the Barclays' Bank Holloway Road branch.

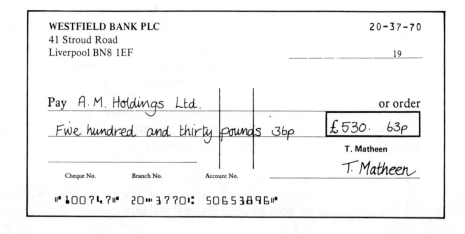

Exercise 39

Put the correct future continuous, future perfect simple, or future perfect continuous tenses into the following sentences which are part of a 'phone conversation between Mr. Offiah, a bank customer, and Miss Jobe, a bank employee.

Example: 'When you (send us) a cheque?'
'I (post) a cheque tomorrow.'
Answer: 'When **will** you **send** us a cheque?'
'I **will post/will be posting** a cheque tomorrow.'

MR. OFFIAH: 'When you (send)[1] my bank statement?' (use future continuous)
MISS JOBE: 'We (post)[2] statements to customers later next week.'
MR. OFFIAH: 'I put a cheque for $2000 in my account three days ago, you (credit)[3] to my account by now?'
MISS JOBE: 'Yes, it (pass)[4] through our clearing system by now.'
MR. OFFIAH: 'I need my statement because I (write)[5] several cheque in the next few days, so I'll want to know my balance.'
MISS JOBE: 'Well, if I make it 'urgent', by this time on Thursday you (receive)[6] it.'
MR. OFFIAH: 'Thursday's no good. I (leave)[7] this country by then, and I (travel)[8] in Europe for the next few weeks, that's why I (write)[9] cheques over the next few days, to pay my bills.'
MISS JOBE: 'Oh, where you (go)[10] to?'
MR. OFFIAH: 'I (stay)[11] in Germany for a week, then I (travel)[12] through France, Italy, and Switzerland, and I (spend)[13] a few weeks in Norway. But that's in the future, I'm interested in my statement now.'
MISS JOBE: 'You (come)[14] to the town centre before you leave?'
MR. OFFIAH: 'I (come)[15] in on Wednesday, I think.'
MISS JOBE: 'We can have it ready at 3.00 on Wednesday, can you pick it up then?'
MR. OFFIAH: 'At three o'clock? Yes, I (finish)[16] all the other things I want to do by then. Yes, I'll pick it up on Wednesday.'
MISS JOBE: 'Come to the counter. I (make)[17] arrangements for the statement to be collected there. If I don't see you, have a nice trip.'
MR. OFFIAH: 'Thank you. Goodbye.'

6.2 Post Office payment and banking services

In the United Kingdom and many other countries the Post Office offers both payment and banking services:

Payment	*National Girobank*
Postage stamps	Current account cheque cards
Cash on delivery (COD)	Deposit account
Postal orders	Loans
Telegraphed money orders	Standing orders
	Statements

Payments

Postage stamps can be used for internal (domestic) payments for small amounts, although in the UK **postal orders** are more commonly used, as these can be bought for amounts from 25p up to £10 with a Post Office charge called 'poundage' added to the amount of the postal order.

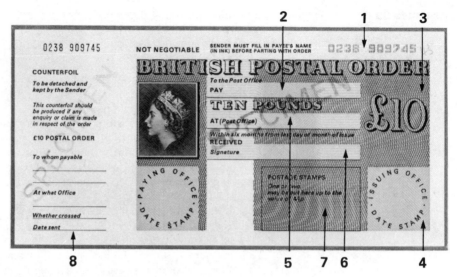

Fig. 44 A British postal order (*Reproduced by kind permission of the Post Office*)

The UK postal order (PO) in fig. 44 shows:

1 The number of the PO which can be quoted if it is lost.
2 The name of the payee (the person receiving the money), but this can be left blank, and they will fill it in before cashing it
3 The value of the order
4 The stamp of the post office which issued (sold) the PO
5 The post office at which it should be cashed; the name of the nearest town or village will do if necessary
6 The signature of the payee
7 Postage stamps of up to 4½p can be added to increase the value of the PO
8 The counterfoil is kept, as it is in a cheque book, to show who received the PO, and whether it was crossed. Like a cheque, a PO can be crossed to make sure that it only goes through a bank account

Cash on delivery (COD)

In the UK post offices will arrange for money to be collected for goods up to the value of £350, with the postman collecting the money.

The sender fixes a label to the package giving the name and address of the person receiving the goods, as well as his/her own name and address. The amount to be collected, and the reference number of the despatch note.

Telegraphed money orders

These can be bought at post offices for values of up to £100 and used inland or for overseas payments. A Post Office form is completed by the sender who pays the cost of the Girocheque (the value of the money order) and Post Office charges. The person receiving the money can then cash it at a post office. Money orders can be crossed, like postal orders and cheques so they can only be cashed through a bank.

National Girobank

The National Girobank in the UK offers most banking facilities and in some cases is cheaper to use than the clearing banks. It offers current account services with cheque books and cards and deposit account and savings accounts services. Standing order payments can be arranged and there are facilities for account holders to get loans.

Transferring cash from one Girobank account to another is done by filling in a transfer/deposit form with the Girobank number of the payee and details of payment, then sending it to Girobank centre in Bootle, Lancashire.

If the payee does not have a Girobank account, a crossed Girobank cheque can be sent direct and he can pay it into his account. If he does not have a bank account, an uncrossed Girobank cheque is sent to Girobank centre and will be cleared and sent on to the payee. For amounts over £50, the payer names a post office where the cheque can be cashed.

Transcash slips are used to pay people with Girobank accounts, see fig. 45. However, if the account number is not known, there is a Girobank Directory where it can be found.

Girobank cheques (fig. 46) can be paid direct to payees just as an ordinary cheque can, and there are facilities for international payments for countries on the Girobank system.

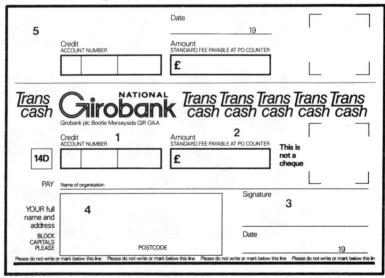

Fig. 45 A Girobank transcash slip (*Reproduced by courtesy of Girobank plc*)

1. Payee's Girobank Account Number (can be found in Girobank Directory)
2. Amount in figures
3. Signature of sender
4. Name and address of sender
5. Counterfoil for reference of payment details
On back of slip there is space for details of payment

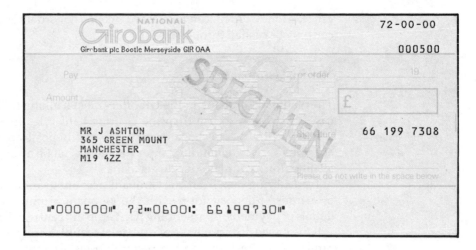

Fig. 46 A Girobank cheque (*Reproduced by courtesy of Girobank plc*)

Exercise 40

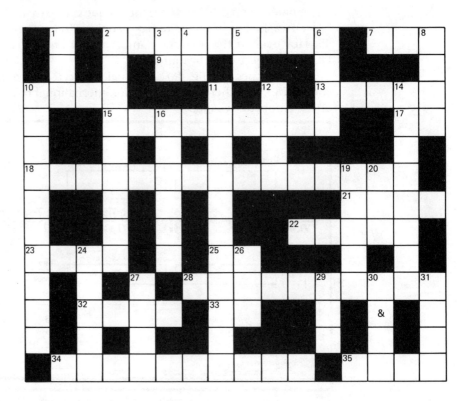

Across

2 Your bank will sent it monthly or quarterly (9)
7 Third person possessive (3)
9 Preposition of direction (2)
10 A programme or scheme (4)
13 To put something ———— until later (5)
15 Outside the bank it will give you money (4) and (5)

17 Preposition which is not 'out' (2)
18 A company will want it if you apply for a job (10) and (5)
21 Eaten a lot in Asia (4)
22 To begin (5)
23 You can put papers in it, or take them out whenever you need them (4)
25 Because (2)
28 Paper, envelopes, pens, and paper-clips etc. (10)
32 Another verb for 'taking money from the bank' (4)
33 If it is not a man or woman we can use this pronoun (2)
34 It tells you your goods are on the way (6) and (4)
35 Even if you don't like someone you would have to begin a letter with this (4)

Down
1 Every one of them (3)
2 If you begin a letter with the person's name, this is how you end it 'Yours ——
———————————————' (9)
3 Preposition of place (2)
4 It's that preposition of direction again (2)
5 It's not your house, its ———— house (2)
6 It's not this one here, it's ———— one there (4)
8 The perfect of 'see' (4)
10 We quote discounts in it (10)
11 You'll have to fill this out if you want the job (11)
12 We use it in microfiche filing systems (4)
14 He's on the Board of the company (8)
16 It's safe! (6)
19 To do the job properly you'll have to ———— for it (5)
20 Goods can be sent by road, rail, sea, and this too (3)
24 He didn't take it away, he ———— it up (5)
26 The past of sit, and an abbreviation for the sixth day of the week (3)
27 Call one if you're in a hurry, but it's expensive (4)
29 It's less than two (3)
30 You see it on invoices and statements to show that mistakes can be corrected (1) and (1) (1)
31 The pen and book belong to you, so they're ———— things (4)

Petty cash

Petty cash means 'small money', and is used to pay small amounts for minor (little) expenses such as pens, taxi or bus fares, small postage items such as a few stamps, or notebooks etc.

The system used for keeping petty cash is called the **imprest** system, imprest meaning 'loans' or 'advances'. It is usually handled by a secretary or office manager so that the Chief Cashier or Accountant does not have to trouble with the small day-to-day expenses of the office.

With the imprest system a fixed amount of money is given to the person in charge of the petty cash, this is called a 'float' which could be, say, $100. As people claim expenses the float, kept in a cash box in a safe, gets less. At the end of the week there may only be $15 left, so on Friday, or the following Monday, $85 will be added to the cash box to bring it back to $100 again.

People who want to be 'reimbursed' (paid back for expenses they have had for the company) go to whoever is in charge of the petty cash and fill out a petty cash voucher, fig. 47, and make out the details of their expenses, and if possible attach a receipt to the voucher. The details of the vouchers are then entered in a petty cash book, and this will be checked by the Chief Cashier, or Accountant every week when s/he 'makes up' the 'float' for the coming week.

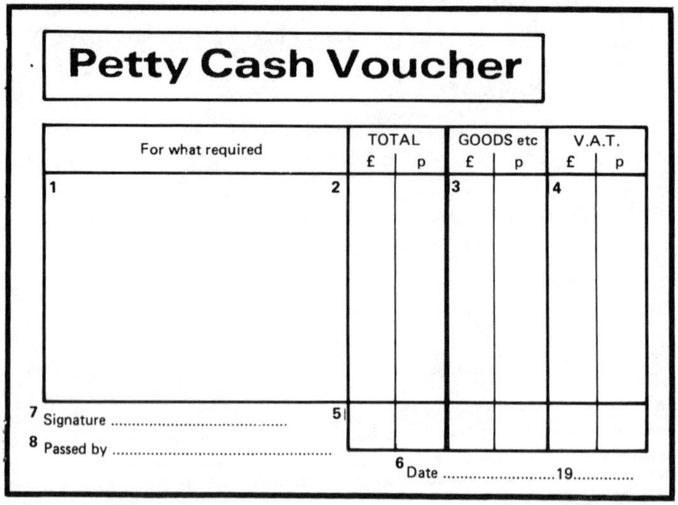

For what required	TOTAL £	p	GOODS etc £	p	V.A.T. £	p
1	2		3		4	
7 Signature 5						
8 Passed by						
	6 Date ....19............					

Petty Cash Voucher

Fig. 47 A petty cash voucher

1 Brief description of the goods bought, or expenses, e.g. 'two cups for office', or 'fares from . . . to . . .'
2 Gross (total) cost of the goods or expenses
3 Net cost of the goods (without tax)
4 Tax on the goods
5 Total columns, as there may be a few different expenses to be added up
6 Date the petty cash is paid. Some companies number their petty cash vouchers for filing
7 Signature of person claiming the money
8 Signature of person allowing the expenses, or giving the petty cash

7.2 The petty cash book and petty cash analysis

Petty cash day books are made up of 'analysis sheets' where items are analysed in columns under titles of the expenses, e.g. travel, stationery etc. There will always be a column marked 'miscellaneous' for goods or expenses which cannot be put under a particular title. The office might have bought cups or flowers or a particular magazine, and these expenses would go under the miscellaneous column (see fig. 48, column (6)).

At the beginning of the week, last week's cash balance is written in, $15, plus the money received to bring the amount back to the weekly 'float' of $100, i.e. $85, see (1).

The date of expenses is entered (1a), and details that appear on the petty cash voucher (2). The voucher number might also be entered (3).

The 'Total paid out' (4) will include the cost of the goods and tax, which like the petty cash voucher in fig. 47 is separate, entered here under VAT (value added tax) column (9).

PETTY CASH ACCOUNT

Dr | | | | | | | | | | Cr

(1) Received	(1a) Date 198-	(2) Details	Fo	(3) V No.	(4) Total paid out	(5) Stationery	(6) Miscellaneous	(7) Travelling	(8) Postage	(9) VAT
15 –	May 10	Balance b/d								
85 –	"		25							
	" 11	Ball Pens			5 –	4 50				50
	" 11	Flowers			7 –		6 –			1 –
	" 12	Magazine			1 20		1			20
	" 12	Fares			7 –			7 –		– –
	" 13	2 Cups			6 50		6 –			50
	" 14	Stamps			9 –				9 –	– –
	" 15	Envelopes			4 50	3 –				1 50
			(10)		40 20	7 50	13 –	7 –	9 –	3 70
			(11)		59 80					
100 –					100 –	S1	S2	T3	P5	T3
	(12)					(14)				
59 80	" 17	Balance b/d								
40 20	" 17	(13) (15)	25							

Fig. 48 A petty cash analysis sheet

The 'Total' column is a running total and the final amount should agree with the gross total of all the other items, e.g. $40.20 (10), and this is deducted (taken away) from the weekly total of $100 to give a balance of $59.80, (11), which is carried down to the next week (12), and the difference is made up to $100 again (13).

At the end of each analysis column there are figures and letters showing that the total amounts have been transferred to their ledger cards in the whole accounting system (14), e.g. P5 will be transferred to the postage account.

In the column marked 'Fo' (15) the folio number of the cash book from which the imprest was transferred is recorded.

Exercise 41

Put the correct **prepositions** in the spaces:

. . .[1] the imprest system a fixed amount . . .[2] money is given . . .[3] the person . . .[4] charge . . .[5] petty cash. The money is kept . . .[6] a cash box and given . . .[7] anyone who has expenses . . .[8] behalf . . .[9] the company and fills . . [10] a petty cash voucher to claim back the money.

. . .[11] the end . . .[12] the week, the float is made . . .[13] again . . .[14] its original amount, and the vouchers are sent . . .[15] the Chief Cashier . . .[16] the analysis sheet . . .[17] that sheet s/he will write . . .[18] the total amounts . . .[19] the ledger cards that relate . . .[20] the particular items, and miscellaneous items will be written . . .[21] . . .[22] a general account used . . .[23] for that purpose.

Exercise 42

Look back at fig. 48 and say where you would put the following:
Example: Fares from office to our factory – under (7) travelling
1　$2.60 for sending parcel
2　Two copies of 'International Trade Journal'
3　Taxi to deliver package to head office
4　Scrap Pad for $6.50, $1.50 of which was tax
5　$82.00 imprest at beginning of week
6　Book of stamps for local mail
7　Replacement of two broken plates @ $7.00 each, $1.20 tax for each
8　$54.00 balance to be carried down to next week's petty cash
9　Folio number of each book
10　Typewriter ribbon for $8.00, 10% tax included in price
11　Cost of sending parcel COD
12　Type-eradicating fluid, $3.00, 15% tax included in price
13　$10.00 train ticket
14　Christmas wrapping paper for parcel
15　Voucher number '31'

Mail

The post room is the centre, in a company, for collecting and distributing (delivering) incoming mail and handling outgoing post.

In a large company the post room might have electric letter openers and sealers, to fold and seal letters, a franking machine, for automatic stamping of outgoing mail, a photocopier for duplicating mail to be distributed to all departments, wire trays for sorting, pigeon holes, a group of boxes, for holding mail until it is distributed and trolleys to wheel round the offices when delivering letters and parcels.

Incoming mail

When mail comes into the post room, it should be opened carefully so its contents are not damaged. If there is no automatic letter opener, a paper knife can be used.

Once the envelope is opened it should be checked inside for 'enclosures' such as documents, cheques, postal orders, or money orders. A quick look at the letter will tell you if there are any enclosures as the bottom of the letter will have a reference to them, e.g. 'Encl.' which means 'enclosure' or the plural 'Encls.'

If the letter says that something has been sent, yet there is nothing in the envelope, make a note and attach it to the correspondence with your initials and mark that it has been sent from the post room in case the receiver wants to contact you.

Most companies 'date stamp' their incoming mail for reference, and at one time letters used to be registered in a mail book, although this is unusual nowadays.

The address on the envelope should tell you who the letter is for, but if the department is not marked, or there is no name, the opening of the correspondence will tell you and there may be an 'attention line' which will say 'Attention Mr. L. Day.' or 'For the attention of . . .'

Most post rooms have a guide to the company's departments and who works in them. If there are any problems, you can check who the letter is from, and from there you can find out who deals with that particular correspondence.

Personal and confidential mail

Some letters are marked 'personal' or 'confidential' on the envelope. These should not be opened, but delivered directly to the person they are addressed to. If it is opened accidentally, a note should be attached and signed explaining the letter was accidentally opened.

Enclosures

Documents and cheques etc., should be attached to the letter they have been sent with by paper clip. Some companies want all money receipts to be entered into a receipt book.

Sorting

Mail can be divided into first and second class post. Sorting can be done with the help of wire trays for different departments, or pigeon holes, putting letters into a group of marked boxes until they are ready to be delivered. If more than one internal post round delivery is necessary, then first class post should be given priority (importance), as second class post could just be circulars (advertisements), or less important correspondence.

Interdepartmental mail

In large companies departments correspond with one another within the organisation. This correspondence takes the form of memorandums – internal notes explaining changes in the company, instructions, announcements of retirements or new staff joining etc., reports – details of developments in the company or information about projects. This sort of internal mail is circulated (handed round) in 'chain envelopes', large brown manila envelopes with lists of staff written on the outside. As the person noted sees the correspondence, they cross out their name and put the 'chain envelope' into an 'out basket' where it is collected then passed on to the next person on the list, see fig. 49.

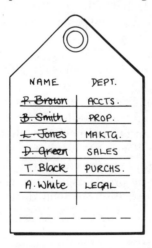

NAME	DEPT.
P. Brown	ACCTS.
B. Smith	PROP.
L. Jones	MAKTG.
D. Green	SALES
T. Black	PURCHS.
A. White	LEGAL

Fig. 49 A chain envelope

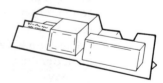

Fig. 50 A letter opening machine

Fig. 51 A paper knife

8.2 Outgoing mail

Outgoing mail generally comes into the post room ready for sending. If it does not the letters have to be folded by hand and put into their envelopes, or some companies have a folding machine.

A quick look at the address on the envelope will tell you if it has been addressed correctly. Be careful with 'window envelopes', which show the address through a cut out section in the envelope: make sure the address is showing, and can be read clearly.

Late afternoon is the busiest time for post rooms as this is when most departments send down their correspondence for posting. Most companies have a final time for 'last mail' to allow the post room to handle all the mail that is going to be sent.

Stamping and franking

As postage rates change quite often the Post Office in your country will supply a 'Post Office Guide' which can be used for reference for regulations about domestic and overseas posting, and leaflets are available in post offices to tell customers about the latest changes in postal rates or rules for sending mail.

In the UK and many other countries there are two classes of postal rate, first and second class, the difference being the time the correspondence takes to reach its destination.

Direct mail, (circulars, leaflets etc.) is sent by second class post, as it is cheaper. More important correspondence goes first class.

Letters and packages should be weighed to work out the postage rate as a wrong stamp will mean the receiver will have to pay double the rate when it is delivered. Most post rooms have scales.

Stamps can be bought in sheets from the post office, but generally large companies have **franking machines**.

Fig. 52 A franking machine and weighing scales

Franking machines are bought or hired from their manufacturers and users are licensed by the Post Office.

The machine is set for the amount of the postage, then the letter is passed through it and franked (stamped) with the value, the date, and the place the letter has come from. The company may also have an advertisement printed along with the postage rate.

Franking machines have a 'descending meter' showing the deductions each time the machine is used, and an 'ascending meter' which increases with each franked impression.

A control card is sent to the Post Office weekly giving the readings of these meters, and it is because of them that 'franked mail' is often called 'metered mail'.

Wrongly franked envelopes must be kept so the Post Office can give the user a refund.

For parcels and packages a gummed strip of paper (sticky on one side) can be drawn through the machine for franking, then stuck onto the package.

Fig. 53 A franked window envelope with advertisement

8.3 The postage book

A postage book records letter and parcel details and costs set against a balance of money that is held by the person in charge of the post-room, or the person responsible for petty cash.

The book is very much like a petty cash book and works on the **imprest system**.

1   The 'addressee' is the name and address of the person receiving the letter or parcel.

2   Postage details give information about how the mail was sent. Here, there are two airmail letters, a 'registered letter', which is a special postal service guaranteeing the safety and delivery of the package or letter, and a 'Datapost' packet, which guarantees delivery anywhere in the world within 24 hours.

Stamps bought		Addressee ①	Stamps used	Postage details ②
$	Date		$	
18·00 ③	June 1	Balance ᵇ/d		
32·00	" 1	Float		
	" 2	A e B Roberts New York USA		Airmail
	2	The Mipune Co. Tokyo	3·10	Airmail
	2	Rockwalls - London	2·50	Registered
	3	H.K. Trading - Hong Kong	15·00	Data Post
	4	Nigerian Importers Lagos	10·20	Parcel Post
	5	L.S. Mair (Local)	— 50	Letter
			32 - 50	
		Balance ᶜ/f	17 - 50 ④	
50·00			50 - 00	
⑤				
17·50	June 8	Balance ᵇ/d		
32·50	" 8	Float		

Fig. 54 A postage book

3 The 'balance brought down (b/d)' is the balance of stamps not used the previous week, and made up by the interest, the advance of $32 which gives the total 'float' of $50.

4 The 'balance carried forward (c/f)' of $17.50 is the stamps left over, and this begins the new week.

Exercise 43

Put **a, the** or leave the spaces **blank** in the following piece:

—— **1**mail (generally) coming into —— **2**post room should be opened carefully; if —— **3**company has —— **4**automatic letter opener, use it, or use —— **5**paper knife.

When you open —— **6**envelope, check it, as there may be —— **7**documents, or —— **8**cheque inside —— **9**envelope. —— **10**people do not realise that ——**11** damaged ——**12**cheque or —— **13**document can mean hours or days of extra work for —— **14**people in —— **15**department which will deal with —— **16**damaged correspondence.

—— **17**paper tears easily, particularly —— **18**paper used for —— **19**airmail letters, so a lot of —— **20**care has to be taken when opening —— **21**correspondence from overseas places like —— **22**USA, —— **23**USSR, —— **24** Africa, or ——**25** Japan.

—— **26**supervisor, or —— **27**head of —— **28**department —— **29**letter was meant for would not like to have to ask —— **30**staff there to waste —— **31**time in writing again for —— **32**same thing to be sent. And if —— **33**correspondence is from —— **34**large organisation like —— **35**United Nations, or —— **36**World Bank, it could take —— **37**long time to get —— **38**same document posted again. Apart from which —— **39**time —— **40**paper —— **41**and —— **42**postal charges are expensive.

Exercise 44   The first group of words are things you would find in a post room, the second group are the jobs they would do. Match the two groups together:

Example: 1 typewriter   (a) filing   (b) writing letters   (c) taking messages.
Answer: 1 (b)

1 transparent sticky tape   2 paper knife   3 franking machine   4 date
stamp   5 paper clip   6 photocopier   7 'chain envelope'
8 trolley   9 wire trays   10 air mail sticker   11 pigeon holes
12 second class stamps   13 postage book   14 corrugated paper
15 gummed strips of paper   16 unused franked envelope   17 stamp float

(a) taking mail round to different departments
(b) stamping outgoing mail
(c) wrapping fragile articles
(d) fixing on overseas mail
(e) recording stamps used every week
(f) using with franking machine for parcels
(g) circulating papers to different departments
(h) fixing loose documents together
(i) opening letters coming into the company
(j) temporarily holding incoming mail before distribution
(k) duplicating internal memos
(l) repairing torn parcels
(m) sorting mail
(n) used to claim postage refund from Post Office
(o) used for sending out circulars and less important mail
(p) weekly advance for stamps to be used
(q) dating incoming mail

8.4 Postal services   In the UK the *Post Office Guide*, which is a book in two volumes, gives details of the regulations for posting internal and overseas mail. However, the following unit explains some of the mail services the UK post office provides and these are generally offered by overseas postal services.

Two-tier card and letter service

There is a first and second class postage rate in the UK. Second class mail generally taking about three days to be delivered in the UK. For bulk mail, over 4 000 letters, the Post Office allows a rebate (a discount) for second class mail.

Newspapers, printed papers, and small packets are delivered as second class mail at special rates provided the newspapers come from publishers or their agents, and printed papers and packets must not have any messages sent with them.

Parcels

Parcel post handles mail up to 22.5kg, and the post offices prefer addresses to be written on the parcel itself, as well as labels, and inside. There is a special **carriage forward** service, where the receiver pays for postage.

Special mail services

Special Delivery services allow mail to be delivered from post offices, by messengers and should arrive the following working day. A label, fig. 55, identifies that the mail is for special delivery.

Certificate of Posting for
Royal Mail Special Delivery ___F 727091___

Note: *See over for conditions of acceptance and instructions, and note about* MONEY *and* JEWELLERY.

Enter below in ink the name and address as written on the letter or packet.

Date stamp

Name

Address

Accepting Officer's Initials

P 3453   Item Code 482850 8/80 56-0455-41C HB

RMSD   Date rec'd in Delivery Office   Date and time of Posting   **Royal Mail Special Delivery**

F 727091

Fig. 55 A special delivery slip

Z 673735   **Recorded Delivery**

Certificate of Posting for Recorded Delivery

How to post

1 Enter below in ink the name and full address as written on the letter or packet.
2 Affix the numbered adhesive label in the top left-hand corner of the letter (or close to the address on a packet).
3 Affix postage stamps to the letter for the correct postage and Recorded Delivery fee.
4 Hand this certificate, together with the letter, to an officer of The Post Office.
5 This certificate will be date-stamped and initialled as a receipt. Please keep it safely, and produce it in the event of a claim.

Name

Address

Postcode

Recorded Delivery should not be used for sending money or valuable items.

For Post Office use   Date stamp

Accepting Officer's initials

Recorded Delivery no.

Z 673735

P2297 Apr 84

Fig. 56 A recorded delivery slip
Label fixed to letter or package
Record of who the package or letter has been sent to, stamped and initialled by the post office clerk and returned to sender

(Illustrations on pages 91 and 92 reproduced by kind permission of the Post Office)

Recorded Delivery is used to prove that mail has been posted and received. A record of sending is handed over the counter to the postal clerk with the extra fee for this special service, and for an extra charge the sender can get a certificate of delivery. On receiving the parcel, letter, or packet, the addressee (the receiver) signs a receipt book handed to him/her by the postman.

Registered letters with money or valuables in them, up to a limit, can be sent through the Post Office, provided the package is sealed with wax or an adhesive (sticking agent). Insurance for the package can also be taken out so that the sender will be compensated if the package is lost, or the post is delayed and s/he loses money through the delay or loss.

Datapost offers a special delivery service anywhere in the world by road, rail, or sea, with the addressee collecting the mail at an agreed time. Charges are based on weight, distance, collection time and delivery.

Railway letters are sent at first class rates plus extra for the letter to be sent on the first available train and posted immediately it enters the station or left to be called for. **Railway parcels** can be given to express delivery post offices who will send a messenger to the nearest station to put on the train. Senders pay the messenger for the parcel delivery and postage.

8.5 Overseas mail

All-up service is for letters and cards going to Europe and these are sent by air or sea, whichever is faster. The blue **Airmail** or **Par avion** sticker, fig. 57, is not necessary. However, mail can be sent by the Swiftair service which ensures overseas letters get to their destinations faster than airmail services. The **Swiftair**, or **Exprès** sticker, fig. 58, distinguishes them from ordinary airmail service.

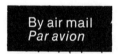

Fig. 57 An air mail sticker

Fig. 58 A Swiftair sticker

Overseas packages must be packed so that they can be opened by customs officers easily, and the customs clearance forms for different types of goods are available from post offices.

Intelpost, in the UK, allows **facsimiles** (fax) of documents to be telegraphed to certain post offices inside the UK and to certain places abroad. These facilities for transferring copies of documents by fax machines are also available in most countries in the world.

Mail collection

In most countries mail can be collected by the Post Office who will rent a box with a box number. But the person hiring the box must give their own private name and address:

B.G. Anders AB,   C & D Ltd.
Box 561   Jabal Amman
201 20 Malmö   PO Box 5171
Sweden   Amman
                                   Jordan

Mail is only handed over to callers if they produce an accepted identity card.

Poste restante, which means 'post waiting', is used for people travelling and not staying at one address for very long. This service allows them to pick up post, with identification, from any post office in the world. Mail must have an address and the words **Post restante** or **to be called for** written on it. Letters must be collected within two weeks, parcels and packets within a month, otherwise they will be returned to the senders.

8.6 Business reply and Freepost

These services are designed for businesses and advertisers who want replies to their advertisements and correspondence, but prefer to pay for the reply. With a **business reply service** the sender encloses an unstamped reply card, envelope folder, or label which the addressee can use without paying postage when answering. **Freepost** works in a similar way with the addressee returning a card with the sender's special address on it.

Senders using either system need a special licence to make use of the service and pay postage on replies and a fee for the use of the service.

Businesses or private people can also ask the Post Office to redirect mail to them by filling in a form giving their old and new addresses, if they move, and paying a redirection fee.

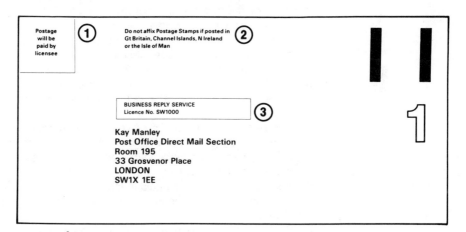

Fig. 59 A business reply card

1 Postage paid by sender
2 Limit on area card can be sent in
3 Licence No. given by Post Office to company using the service

Finally, we might also mention that there are now many private courier (delivery and collection) services competing with the Post Office and offering fast personal internal and overseas letter and parcel services.

Exercise 45

Choose the correct answer from (a), (b), (c):
1 Carriage forward means (a) the sender, (b) the receiver, (c) the Post Office pays for postage.
2 An 'all-up' service is for letters and cards going to (a) South East Asia, (b) America, (c) Europe.
3 If a company has a 'box number' they will (a) collect their mail at the post office, (b) have their mail forwarded to them, (c) not pay for replies to advertisements.
4 When a company uses 'Freepost' services they (a) have their mail delivered by special courier, (b) have their mail sent first class, (c) pay postage for replies.
5 Letters and packets sent by 'recorded delivery' offer the sender (a) proof that the mail has been received, (b) proof that the mail has been sent, (c) proof that mail has been received and sent.
6 'Intelpost' in the UK allows (a) copies of documents to be sent through a machine, (b) senders to get a reply within 24 hours, (c) addressees to receive documents within 24 hours.
7 Travelling businessmen who will not stay for long in one place would use (a) Poste restante services, (b) box numbers, (c) special delivery services, to collect their mail
8 In the UK there is/are (a) one, (b) two, (c) three class(es) of post for letters.
9 The charge for the 'Datapost' service in the UK is based on (a) weight, (b) weight and distance, (c) weight, distance, and collection time plus delivery.
10 If a firm sends over 4 000 letters the Post Office will (a) allow a discount on second class mail, (b) not allow a discount on second class mail, (c) will allow a discount on first and second class mail.

Exercise 46

Change the following sentences into the **passive**, and use the agent where it is necessary.
Example: You made a mistake (active)
Answer: A mistake **was made** (passive)
1 You made a mistake when you wrote out the invoice. You overcharged us, so you must send us a credit note.
2 All our customers allow us a 10% discount when we buy goods in bulk.
3 Staff must not use the canteen while the decorators are decorating it.
4 Customers must show a cheque card when they are paying for goods by cheque.
5 People say that the Post Office services are more reliable than private courier service. People say that the Post Office is also cheaper. But some people say that because private courier services have less work to deal with, they can be more efficient.
6 You must take these parcels to the Post Office. You must send them by registered post. Someone must sign for them, and you have to bring back the receipt.
7 Someone took my pen, and when I asked who took it, no one answered my question, but someone is using it in this office.
8 Girobank offers a full banking service. Customers can use chequebook facilities, and they can transfer payments through the Girobank system. They can save money through savings accounts, and Girobank gives interest on the accounts.
9 Instructions for using a photocopier:
   You press the button marked 'on'. You allow the machine to warm up. You put the paper in the 'feed tray', you put the document you are photocopying over the glass panel. You close the cover. You set the dial

to the number of copies you want, then you press the button marked 'start', then you wait until the machine finishes the 'run'.

10 Talking about a repair to a photocopier:

'The machine broke down yesterday, and someone called the service department. When they came, they took the machine apart, and they examined every piece in it. Then they put in a new drum, and they filled the machine with 'toner'. They said that someone had been using the wrong sized paper.'

Stationery

9.1 Equipment

We have already mentioned a number of stationery items used in different areas of office practice, and these are included in the following list which could be found in most companies' stationery stores:

Clips: bulldog-clips for holding thick wads of papers, and paper clips to hold a few papers together.

Carbons: to make copies of correspondence and documents on typewriters or in receipt books.

Duplicating papers and inks: used for machines to 'run off' (produce) hundreds or thousands of copies of memorandums, reports, or leaflets.

Folders: which are used in all areas of filing to hold documents and papers.

Gums and glues: adhesives used for sticking labels and tags onto boxes, files, folders, etc.

Punches: to make holes in papers for filing.

Rubber bands: elastic bands for holding things together.

Stamps and pads: for date stamping and identifying documents.

Stencils: special paper which can be cut through so that it can be fitted to a duplicator to run off hundreds of copies.

String and paper: for wrapping parcels.

Typewriting materials: carbons, papers, erasers, ribbons and cassettes.

Writing materials: pens, ball points, pencils, felt tipped pens, erasers, writing pads for making notes, jotters or note pads for quick messages, rulers, squares, and folders.

You will also find drawing pins and coloured pins for fixing notices to boards and making wall charts, cassettes for 'dictaphones', machines that record dictated letters for typists to copy from, equipment for filing, sticky tape for repairing files, tabs and tags and labels, and even computer software – the material used in making computer programs and paper output.

9.2 Paper and envelopes

Probably the main items a stationery store issues (gives out) are paper and envelopes.

There are four different types of paper a company could use:

Bond – good quality paper used for top copies (originals) and which usually has the company's heading (its name and address) at the top of it

Bank – light, flimsy (thin) paper for typed copies

Duplicating paper – which takes ink when used with a stencil on a duplicating machine

NCR (no carbon required) *paper* – which is often lined up for accounting documents such as invoices, delivery notes, statements etc.

The metric system has meant that paper sizes have become almost standard (the same) all over the world from the largest size A0 used for posters, to A4, the most commonly used size for business letters and reports, down to A7 used for visiting cards.

Fig. 60. gives you an idea of the relationship of paper sizes. Notice that as the numbers increase from A0 to A7 each size is half that of the number before it.

A1   Posters
A2   Notices
A3   Legal documents,
       financial statements
A4   Letters, reports,
       commercial documents
A5   Memos, invoices,
       statements etc.
A6   Postcards, index cards,
       petty cash vouchers
A7   Visiting cards, labels

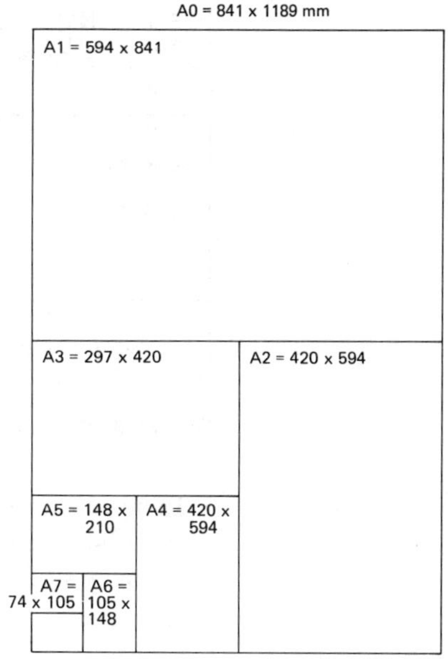

A0 = 841 x 1189 mm
A1 = 594 x 841
A3 = 297 x 420
A2 = 420 x 594
A5 = 148 x 210
A4 = 420 x 594
A7 = 74 x 105
A6 = 105 x 148

Fig. 60 International paper sizes

Commercial paper is made to fit standard sized envelopes. Here are some examples of envelopes and the paper they take, the letters and numbers, e.g. C4 are international envelope sizes:

Envelope size in millimetres	unfolded	folded once	folded twice
C3 324 × 458	A3	A2	A1
C4 229 × 324 or B4 250 × 353	A4	A3	A2
C5 162 × 229 or B5 176 × 250	A5	A4	A3
C6 114 × 162 or B6 125 × 324			
C5/6	A6	A5	A4
C7/6 81 × 162			A5

There are three main types of envelopes used in business:

Banker   *Window*

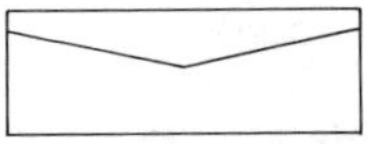

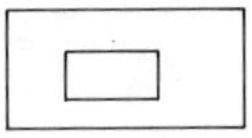

Pocket

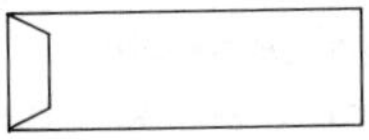

9.3 Organisation of stationery

In a small firm stationery might be kept in a locked cupboard with a secretary given the job of handing it out when it is needed. In larger companies there is a stationery store, usually only open at certain times, which are listed on a memo, and only handing out stationery when the person in charge is given an official **requisition** from a department manager, fig. 61.

STATIONERY REQUISITION From Name of Department To Stationery Store	Job No.______
Quantity	Description
number wanted	Type of stationery
Signed Person collecting the stationery	Date______

Fig. 61 A stationery requisition

In small companies a stationery book is kept to record stocks, purchases of new stationery, and issues (stationery handed out). In larger firms a stationery stock card will be kept, fig. 62.

STATIONERY STOCK CARD

(1) Item Paper Clips

(2) Maximum stock: 12 Minimum stock: 5

Date (3)	Receipts: Quant. received (4)	Receipts: Invoice No. (5)	Receipts: Supplier (6)	Issues: Quantity issued (7)	Issues: Requisition No. (8)	Issues: Department (9)	Balance in stock (10)
Ap 11							8
" 8				1 box	703	Sales	7
" 10				2 boxes	752	Filing	5
May 11				3 boxes	913	Accounts	2
16	10	01345	A&B Stationers Ltd				12

Fig. 62 A stationery stock card

1 Item being recorded on the card. Here it is paper clips, but it could be paper, pens, ribbons etc.
2 Maximum/Minimum stock. This is the maximum number of boxes

1 Item being recorded on the card. Here it is paper clips, but it could be paper, pens, ribbons etc.
2 Maximum/Minimum stock. This is the maximum number of boxes that should be held in store, holding any more would just waste money and space; the minimum number of boxes tells the stationery clerk to order more items if the number in store is below this figure.
3 Date of issue.
4 These columns deal with stationery bought. On May 16, for
5 example 10 boxes of paper clips were bought from A & B Stationers
6 Ltd. under Invoice No. D1345, and this brought the balance of boxes in store (10) to 12.
7 The number of boxes issued to the department needing them.
8 The stationery requisition number for files.
9 The department asking for the stationery supplies.
10 The balance of boxes left in the store-room. On April 1st, there were '8' which went down to '2' by May 11, then brought back to the maximum number to be held on May 16.

Price lists and **specimens** (examples) of stationery should be kept so that items can be easily re-ordered, and an index-card system can be used when doing this. It is often useful when re-ordering to send a sample (an example) of the stationery along so no mistakes are made, and of course, quote any reference numbers.

When ordering 'printed stationery' it is very important to send a specimen along, not only so that the printers will print up the item exactly, but so they will also use the same quality paper. Ledger cards, for example, have to be printed on durable paper (paper that will last a long time) as they are often in use for checking accounts, making statements, entering payments or sales/purchases.

Most large companies buy stationery 'in bulk' (in large quantities) so they can get **bulk discounts**, and it is important for the person checking in deliveries to examine the stationery against the order to make sure the right goods have been delivered.

Exercise 47

Say if the following statements are *true* or *false*:

True   *False*

1 **Bank paper** is used for original copies to be sent out to customers. ☐ ☐
2 A **bank envelope** has a flap on the long side. ☐ ☐
3 The usual size of paper used for business letters is A1. ☐ ☐
4 Carbon papers are used in typewriters to make copies of originals. ☐ ☐
5 Bond paper is a good quality paper which usually has a firm's heading on it. ☐ ☐
6 A stencil is used when duplicating hundreds of copies. ☐ ☐
7 'Bulk buying' means buying just a few items. ☐ ☐
8 A3 paper folded twice, will fit into a C3 envelope. ☐ ☐
9 A1 paper folded once, will fit into a C3 envelope. ☐ ☐

	True	False

10 Cassettes and ribbons are two items used with typewriters.

11 Stationary means 'not moving'.

12 A 'specimen' is an example of something.

13 A bulldog-clip would be used to hold a couple of sheets of paper together.

14 The word 'adhesive' means to stick.

15 A 'pocket envelope' has its flap on the long side of the envelope.

16 A4 paper is half the size of A3 paper.

17 A B5 envelope is about postcard size.

18 A6 paper is about postcard size.

19 When accepting a delivery of stationery you can sign for it 'goods not examined' and check the order later.

20 Stationery means 'not moving'.

Exercise 48

In Exercise 46 you changed the **active voice** into the **passive voice**. Read the piece below then change the **passive** voice into the **active**.

Example: 'I **was** given the pen, by Mary.' (passive)

Answer: 'Mary gave me the pen.' (active)

1 Stationery is bought in bulk by large companies as it is used in large quantities, so discounts are given to the companies by their suppliers. (3 passives)

2 I was told by the manager to get 500 sheets of A4 paper, but when it was given to him I was told I had bought A5 which was too small for use for correspondence. (2 passives)

3 Only five or six copies of an original can be typed by a manual typewriter, however, there is no limit to the number of originals that can be 'run off' by a word processor. (2 passives)

4 Complaint about a wrong delivery.
'We have been sent the wrong order. Two hundred C3 envelopes were ordered, but two thousand have been delivered; can these be collected by your delivery van as the extra envelopes will not be used because we are only a small company.' (5 passives)

5 (a) 'How long were you made to wait for your interview?'
    (b) 'I was made to wait for over an hour before I was seen.'
    (c) 'When you were interviewed, were you asked about your previous experience in an office?'
    (d) 'Oh, yes. I was asked about that, and how long I had been employed by the company I was working for.'
    (e) 'How long were you interviewed for?'
    (f) 'I was not interviewed for long, quite a few other people had to be seen, so I was only interviewed for about twenty minutes.'
    (g) 'Do you think you will be given the job?'
    (h) 'I will be given the job, if the other people who were seen do not have my experience.'
    (i) 'What do you think they were most impressed with?'
    (j) 'My patience in waiting!'

Exercise 49   Office stationery and equipment comes in different shapes and sizes. Can you give a name to these shapes:

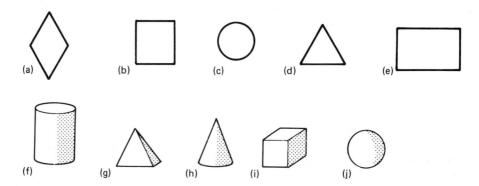

(a)   (b)   (c)   (d)   (e)

(f)   (g)   (h)   (i)   (j)

Exercise 50

| STATIONERY STOCK CARD | | | | | | Maximum stock: 50 reams | |
| Item___A4 Paper___ | | | | | | Minimum stock: 15 reams | |

Date	Receipts			Issues			Balance in stock
	Quantity received	Invoice No.	Supplier	Quantity issued	Requisition No.	Department	
June 1							25

Fill in the information on the above stationery stock card for A4 paper. You can see that the maximum stock is 50 reams (a ream is a packet of 500 sheets of paper) and the minimum is 15 reams. On June 1 there were 25 reams in stock.

June 8   7 reams taken by typing pool on requisition no. 345
June 16   2 reams taken by accounts on requisition no. 451
June 24   3 reams taken by salaries on requisition no. 506
June 25 a number of reams ordered from Modern Stationery Co. Ltd to bring stock back to its maximum number – how many reams have been ordered?

Office machinery

There are four main types of typewriting machines being used in offices at present, **manual, electric** and **electronic typewriters**, and **word processors**.

Manual typewriters

These machines generally have a 14-in (350mm) carriage, although special machines have larger carriages for wider paper needed for accounts, and are limited in the typestyles they use, e.g. pica, or elite:

```
A B C D E F G H I          A B C D E F G H I J
a b c d e f g h i          a b c d e f g h i j
1 2 3 4 5 6 7 8 9          1 2 3 4 5 6 7 8 9 0

      Pica                          Elite
```

The **type pitch** the width of each character is also limited to 10 characters to the inch (2.5cm) for pica, and 12 for elite. As a rule **portable typewriters**, which as their name suggests, mean you can carry them around in a case, also are manual machines, although more electric portables are coming onto the market.

Electric typewriters

These typewriters have almost taken over in most modern offices from manual machines as they are quicker to use, give an even type no matter what pressure the typist uses, can make more carbon copies than manuals, and cut better stencils. They also have 'repeater keys' to automatically type lines, full stops etc., and the carriage return is also automatic which saves the typist time.

The IBM 'golf ball' has its characters round a single arm which itself moves, so there is no carriage movement, and the 'golf ball' can be changed to vary the typefaces.

Electric typewriters also give a wider range of typestyles. The standard carriage length can also be increased up to 26in (650mm) to handle legal documents and accounts work.

Electronic typewriters

These machines have less moving parts than either electric or manual typewriters, and most important have a **memory** which can handle from 20 up to 3 500 characters depending on the model. The more expensive machines can edit (correct and add information) to printed material, or transfer to magnetic cards, discs, and tapes as well as being linked up to a visual display unit (VDU) so you can see what has been stored.

Typefaces are arranged on a 'daisy-wheel', fig. 63, which can be changed very quickly to give a wide range of letters and pitches.

Fig. 63 A daisy wheel

Word processors

Word processors are used with VDUs (screens) and printers which allow typed material to be reproduced again and again in top copies. The operator's work is reproduced on the VDU and information, letters, reports, memos etc., can be stored on discs, magnetic tape or cards for reprinting.

The machines will 'edit', adjust material so that new words or phrases can be put in, or taken out; 'justify margins', adjust margins either side of the page; align material in tabulated form, so that figures or words can be put into columns, and move written material around the full or half page displayed on the screen by moving the 'cursor' (a small square displayed to show the operator where material is being moved to).

Processors have a standard keyboard, with what is called a 'qwerty' layout, like a normal typewriter, but there are additional keys which allow the machine to handle its other functions, e.g. getting information from stored material, aligning, reprinting and adjusting.

Reports, circular letters (standard letters sent to hundreds of customers), lists and revised (updated) information is typed on word processors as they allow 'text' (written information) changes to be made, fig. 65.

Fig. 64 A word processor (*Courtesy of IBM United Kingdom Ltd.*)

Fig. 65 An electronic typewriter *(Courtesy of IBM United Kingdom Ltd.)*
The machine in this illustration will align figures, centre, justify (arrange margins), underline, remember tab settings and help load its own paper. It has a 15 500 character memory and edits texts. It has 25 typestyles in 10 and 12 pitch, a simple error correction device and is available with either a 15.5-inch or 19-inch carriage (394 mm or 485 mm).

Fig. 66 A cartridge ribbon *(Courtesy of IBM United Kingdom Ltd.)*

Accessories for typewriters

Accessories are things that can be used with something else. There are a number of accessories that are used with all models of typewriters.

Ribbons which come in spools, fig. 67 are generally used with manual machines and have to be threaded through the machine. Cassettes, fig. 66 and cartridges, which are already threaded, are used for electric and electronic machines, word processors, and printers and are simply fitted to the machine in their cases. They often have an erasing tape fitted so that errors can be erased (taken out) without the use of whitening fluid (which paints over the error) or chalked paper which types over the error.

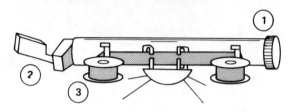

1 Platen (roller)
2 Carriage shift
3 Spool (threaded through by typist)

Fig. 67 A spool

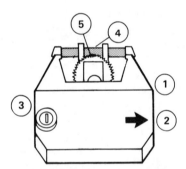

1 Cassette case
2 Indicator to see how much
  ribbon is left
3 Ribbon tightener
4 Ribbon
5 Daisy-wheel

Fig. 68 A cassette

Nylon, silk, and cotton ribbons can be reused, but ribbons in cassettes are often carbon and though they make an excellent impression on the paper they can only be used once.

Backing sheets can also be used with machines, to protect the platen, give the typist a guide to where s/he is working on the paper, and to keep carbons aligned.

Erasing errors can be done by using a rubber, which may be in the form of a 'ring' or 'pencil', but this has to be done carefully with carbon copies, and flakes of rubber usually fall into the machine, or liquid whitener, which paints over the error, or chalk paper to type over the error.

Exercise 51

Grammar

Articles **a/an** *the* **blank**

Here are some instructions for taking care of a typewriter. Put in the articles or leave blank where necessary.

Always cover ——— [1]machine after it has been used to protect it from ——— [2]dust.

Brush ——— [3]machine carefully, and remember to brush ——— [4]underneath as dust rises.

Align ——— [5]carriage when you have finished with ——— [6]machine. ——— [7]carriage sticking out over ——— [8]desk is dangerous to anyone passing and ——— [9]machine itself can be damaged.

Always use ——— [10]backing sheet when typing if there are no ——— [11]carbon copies. ——— [12]work you produce will look better, and ——— [13]platen (——— [14]roller) will be protected.

Lift ——— [15]machine from underneath or slide it off ——— [16]desk towards you to get hold of it.

If ——— [17]machine works on ——— [18]electric power, and does not work, check that ——— [19]plug is connected to ——— [20]the power point. If it still does not work, check that it is 'on'. If there are any further problems, call someone. And if they cannot discover why ——— [21]machine is not working, they will call ——— [22]mechanic. If ——— [23]machine is ——— [24]manual typewriter, check ——— [25]carriage release, which frees ——— [26]carriage. Check ——— [27]paper release is set, if ——— [28]paper does not feed through properly. Check ——— [29]margin space, and ——— [30]'spacing set', which might be on ——— [31]zero. If there is still ——— [32]problem, call ——— [33]someone, or ——— [34]mechanic. Never use ——— [35]water or ——— [36]oil on a typewriter, only use ——— [37]spirit (——— [38]chemical), and then only when someone has shown you how to use it.

Exercise 52

Choose the correct word for the sentences from the list below:

1 The ——— ———is the width of each character.
2 A ——— ——— can be changed very quickly and gives a wide selection of ———.
3 A ribbon on a ——— is used with a manual typewriter.
4 The roller is also called the ———.
5 The two most common typestyles are called ——— and ———.
6 An electronic typewriter has a ——— which can handle from 20 up to 31 500 ———.
7 Word processors have both ——— and ———.
8 A standard letter sent out to hundreds of customers is called a ———.
9 Ribbons in cases are called ——— and ———.
10 ——— ribbons can only be used once.

typestyles   memory   circular   spool   characters   carbon
platen   type pitch   daisy wheel   pica   cassettes   elite   screens
    cartridges   printers

10.2 Audio typing

Many secretaries use shorthand (stenography) to take notes and then translate the script into words which they type. However, an audio machine allows the person 'dictating' the correspondence to put the letter on a tape which can then be 'typed up' later by a secretary or copy-typist (fig. 69).

Most audio machines work on a foot pedal control so the typist's hands are free. Of course her spelling and punctuation must be very good, and her judgement has to be used, sometimes, when the person dictating the correspondence uses bad grammar, or makes a mistake, in, say, figures, when the typist is certain that a mistake has been made. This would have to be checked.

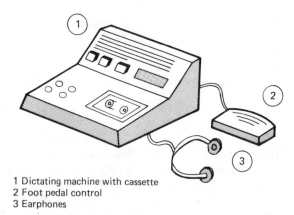

1 Dictating machine with cassette
2 Foot pedal control
3 Earphones

Fig. 69 Audio typing equipment

Stenotyping

This method of shorthand combines typing with stenography (shorthand). The secretary uses the stenomachine instead of a notepad and types phonetic symbols (symbols for the way words sound) and later transcribes (changes into written words) the dictation. Stenotyping machines are used in court rooms and board rooms for fast dictation. They are now combined with word processors and computers.

10.3 Calculators

Calculators range from the small pocket models that run on batteries or solar cells to the larger desk models, fig. 70, that work on batteries or main power sources.

All machines offer the basic functions of adding, subtracting, dividing, multiplying and selecting decimal points. The larger desk machines also offer 'tally rolls' – paper print-outs of calculations – and can be set to give reference numbers for invoices, or credit and debit notes.

In addition to the basic functions many machines have independent memories that will hold a selection of figures, or will repeat them for use in other calculations. They will also work out square roots, percentages, and sign changes.

10.4 Computers

Compute simply means to 'calculate' or 'work out' an answer to a problem, which was the original function (job) of computers.

There are three main types of computers:

Mainframes, very large machines used by big organisations such as insurance offices, banks, and chain stores.

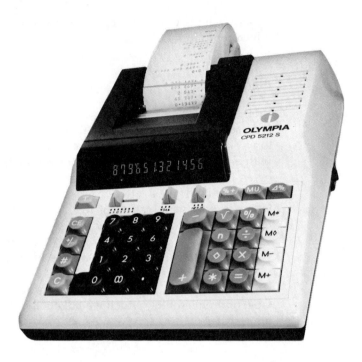

Fig. 70 A desk calculator with paper roll (*Courtesy of Olympia Business Machines*)

Minicomputers, used in stores and on the desks of office staff.

Microcomputers programmed (instructed) by **microprocessors**, which are small silicon chips with circuits printed on them giving a wide range of instructions to a machine like a word processor or video recorder.

Computers need a **program** to work. This is a set of instructions telling the machine in logical steps what to do, because computers cannot 'think'. The program is carefully prepared on a 'flow chart' (a chart of its instructions), which is then translated into the machine's language. Different machines use different languages just as different nationalities do. The most common computer language is BASIC, which stands for Beginner's All Purpose Symbolic Instruction Code. There are different types of BASIC, just as there are different types of Italian and French, and we use the same word for these different types of language – **dialects**.

In science the computer language is FORTRAN (FORmula TRANslation) and for commerce we use COBOL (COmmon Business Oriented Language).

Computers store **data** (information) in their **memory** and this is made to work by the computer's 'brain' called the **central processing unit** (CPU).

Input, the information put into the computer, can be typed on a keyboard, similar to that of a typewriter, or by 'printed cards', 'paper tape', 'magnetic tape' (like that in your cassette at home), or transferred onto objects in 'magnetic ink' (which you will find in numbers on the bottom of a cheque or the back of a book).

The machine works by turning electrical circuits 'on' and 'off' when it is instructed by a special form of arithmetic called the **binary code**, which uses only two digits 1 and 0 to represent any number. But there are other codes which computers can use.

Bits and bytes

Bits (Binary digITS = bits) are individual digits (numbers) and are represented by '1' (a pulse) and '0' (no pulse) and these instruct the machine to work. Eight-bits is called a *byte* (or *word*). An eight-bit computer works with eight-bit words, and computer sizes are indicated by the number of bytes they can hold (the amount of information they hold). An 8-byte computer holds 8000 letters or numbers, a 16-byte computer holds 16 000 letters or numbers. Instead of 1000, the term K is used, so a 16K computer holds 16 000 bytes. A **megabyte** is one million bytes of information about 420 A4 pages.

The **output** of the information, the information the machine gives you, can be shown on a VDU (visual display unit) screen, as we saw with the word processor; on paper in **print-outs** from a machine called a **line-printer**; tape; or on microfilm, which we talked about in the unit on the **microfiche** filing system.

Hardware and software

The **hardware** of a computer is the machinery itself, and the **software**, the programs and the data. One way of thinking of it, is that **hardware**, the CPU or printer, cannot be changed, but software, the program, can be changed.

Holding information and communicating

Backing storage, holding information, can be done on magnetic tapes, or **floppy discs**.

There are minifloppy discs (**minifloppies**) used by microcomputers and holding 100 kilobytes (100K) of information. Microfloppy discs (microfloppies) and standardfloppy discs (**standard floppies**) which are used by large machines. There are also **hard discs** (about 180mm in diameter) which can store 40 times the amount of information of a floppy disc and are used by mainframe computers.

Databases, or **databanks** are central stores of masses of information such as licence numbers, companies' registrations, and government files. Television uses these services on **teletext** services, and the public can phone on a **viewdata** system to get information about weather, sport, or the stock market. Together these systems are known as **videotex**.

Networks of computers link up businesses through **terminals** which can be in the form of VDUs or phones to exchange information. Banks, insurance offices, transport and communications companies usually have terminal networks to exchange instant information.

We can see computers at work every day, in supermarkets and bookshops which use **bar coding** for optical scanning (fig. 72), giving the maker,

Fig. 71 A computer with VDU, keyboard and printer (*Courtesy of IBM United Kingdom Ltd.*)

9 780272 798195

Fig. 72 Bar coding for optical scanning

product, price, and stock replacement order. In banks, where **magnetic ink character recognition** (MICR) systems are used to identify the customer and details of his/her account, fig. 73, and on application and examination forms and papers where pencil and ink marks are picked up by computers using **optical character recognition** (OCR).

⑈573054⑈ 40⑈1840⑈ 00643912⑈

number of your cheque,   number of your branch   and your personal account number.

Fig. 73 MCR coding on a cheque

Exercise 53   Choose the correct word or term from the three given.
   1 The largest of computers used by big organisations are called
      (a) microcomputers (b) mainframes (c) word processors.
   2 The 'brain' of the computer is (a) the central operating unit (b) the main operating
      unit (c) the central processing unit.

3   The most common computer language used in business is (a) FORTRAN
    (b) BASIC (c) COBOL.
4   A 16-byte computer holds (a) 1600 (b) 16 000 (c) 160 000 bits.
5   The **hardware** of a computer (a) can be changed (b) cannot be changed
    (c) can be processed.
6   A **network** of computers links (a) terminals (b) terminates (c) termites.
7   A **viewdata** system gives information by (a) phone (b) television (c) data-
    banks.
8   Megabytes are about (a) 800 (b) 420 (c) 240 pages of A4 information.
9   An example of **software** would be (a) a printer; (b) a CPU; (c) a
    program.
10 (a) Eight (b) ten (c) twelve **bits** make up one **byte**.
11 **Input** is (a) information taken from (b) put into (c) taken over from the
    computer.
12 Discs which hold the most information are called (a) hard discs (b) standard
    floppies (c) minifloppies.
13 Very small computer circuits which operate video recorders are called (a) silicon
    chips (b) microfiche (c) fiche 'n chips.
14 **Videotex** services rely on (a) phone communication (b) screen viewing
    (c) both phone and screen viewing.
15 MICR systems use (a) figures (b) bars (c) pencil marks to identify.

Reprography

In Unit 10 we saw there are a number of ways of reproducing material in a company. Carbon copies can be produced by typewriters, electronic machines handling up to eleven copies at a time. Word processors and computers with printers can also produce large numbers of copies, but this can be expensive with carbon ribbons which can only be used once. Most large companies, therefore, have reprographic equipment which can produce hundreds or thousands of copies comparatively cheaply, and in some organisations there is a special 'Duplicating Section' which is only used for duplicating accounts, documents, circular letters etc.

11.1 Duplicating

This involves the use of **stencils**, the process of cutting letters, figures, or drawings into the paper either with a typewriter, set on 'stencil' (with no ribbon used) so that the keys cut through the special wax tissue of the paper, or with a 'stylus', a steel nib pen, (used without ink) which cuts images into the stencil.

A carbon can be placed between the stencil and its backing sheet so that the typist can see the work that is being produced, and the stencil itself has guides printed on it for positioning of information.

Once the stencil is cut it is put through a duplicating machine which has an inked drum which the stencil is fitted round. The drum can be turned by hand, or power operated and will roll copies off the stencil.

The paper used is absorbent (will take in the ink like a sponge) so the ink dries quickly, and there is no offset impression on the back of it (fig. 74).

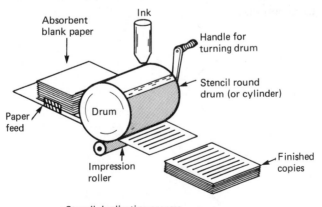

Stencil duplicating process

Fig. 74 Stencil duplicating process

If mistakes are made on the stencil in cutting it, **correcting fluid** can be used. This is a wax-based liquid, usually pinkish, which is painted over the error so it can be re-cut. Stencil paper can also be 'grafted' (cut from another sheet and fixed over the error or damaged paper).

Once the stencil has been 'run off' it should be taken off the duplicator straight away, allowed to dry, then stored either in an old stencil box, or vertical (upright) stencil file.

Stencils are only usually in one colour as different colours mean changing the drum and ink and re-running the programme. But they are cheaper than most methods of reproducing material and with careful handling will give about 5000 copies of an item.

Spirit duplicating

This method uses spirit instead of ink to produce copies, therefore we get the name 'spirit duplicating'.

The **master copy** (the original from which other copies are made) is not cut through, as it is in stencils, but typed, written, or drawn on with a ball point pen, pencil, or sharp pointed instrument.

The master copy is coated with china clay and the backing sheet has an aniline dye on it, like a carbon. The impression comes out in a 'mirror image' (the image you would see of writing in a mirror) and is placed on the drum (cylinder) of the duplicator.

Spirit is added as the machine begins its 'run' and this washes off some of the dye onto the paper being copied, fig. 75. As the carbons of the backing sheets (called **hectograph** carbons) come in different colours it is possible to have a number of different colours on the duplicated sheets, if the master copy is prepared using different carbons in the beginning.

Errors are 'scraped off' the master sheet, and grafting carbon from an old backing sheet allows the error to be corrected. Correcting fluid can also be used to paint over errors. Unlike stencils, the copies do not give a very clear image, will fade in daylight, and only have a run of about 200 copies, so that although the method is cheaper than stencil duplicating, it is usually used for internal correspondence and documents rather than copies being sent to customers.

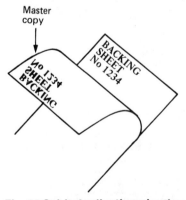

Fig. 75 Spirit duplicating sheets

Offset-litho duplicating

This form of duplicating is used when firms need thousands of copies of the material either for letter headings, catalogues, price-lists, or for printing their own stationery.

Offset means to 'set against', and **litho** is an abbreviation for 'lithography', which means 'printing by stone', which was the way this printing was done two centuries ago. It works on the principle that oil and water do not mix, so the master copy's area for printing is greasy, and this rejects the water used in offset-litho printing. The first impression of the master is taken on a rubber cylinder and is then printed onto paper, although metal plates are also used. The master is rolled onto an inking roller (ink is accepted by the greasy image), which is then offset onto a rubber roller, and again offset onto copy paper (fig. 76).

The paper used is expensive and litho machines are expensive to buy, so they are often hired by companies.

Master paper plates can be prepared by using ball point pens, pencils, or typed with an offset-litho ribbon; however, there is an electrostatic process (using 'static electricity' to attract a dye) which is generally used to prepare master copies.

Metal master plates are prepared with photographic equipment.

Errors on paper are corrected with an offset-litho eraser, and on metal plates with a glass brush or pumice (volcano stone) block.

Paper master copies are rarely stored, but metal plates which are used for thousands of copies have to be specially treated before being stored with a gum seal, and this has to be washed off when they are needed again.

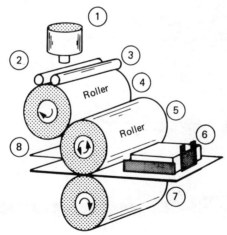

1 Water feed
2 Damping Roller
3 Inking Roller
4 Master plate drum, plate fixed over this cylinder
5 Offset drum, this cylinder has a rubber covering
6 Paper feed
7 Impression drum to create pressure against '5'
8 Finished copies

Fig. 76 Offset litho printing

11.2 Office copying machines

Photocopiers are being used less now as the paper, which was coated in zinc oxide (a chemical), was unpleasant to use, and the liquid toner, which was fused to the paper by a light flash, left the paper damp.

Thermal copiers, using heat to transfer the image, are expensive to use and will only copy inks which have carbon in them (e.g. typewriter ribbons, fountain pen ink, fibre tipped pens).

Electrostatic copying uses static electricity (the electricity you get if you rub nylon substances) to fuse a 'dry toner' (like a powdered black ink) onto bond paper. So where the original is dark there is an image and where it is light, there is no image.

As the paper is not specially treated it is cheaper than other copying methods, and machines can be controlled to reduce the size of the copies.

11.3 Collators

These machines save the trouble of spreading out hundreds of copies over desks to sort them into numbered pages. The stacks of papers are put into shelves which will then automatically feed papers into their groups. In fig 77, the copier has a collating machine fixed under it, and will automatically collate reproduced material.

Fig. 77 A copier and collator (*Courtesy of IBM United Kingdom Ltd.*)

Exercise 54

Use the **correct tenses, conditionals**, or **reported speech** in the following conversation. The comments at the end of the sentences will help you.
Example: 'It (be) cheaper, if I (use) a stencil.'
          'So (use) you a stencil?' (intention)
          'No I (do) this on the photocopier.' (intention)

Answer: 'It **would be** cheaper, if I **used** a stencil.'
'So **are** you **going to use** a stencil?'
'No I'**m doing** this on the photocopier.'

NANCY: 'What (do)**¹** with these documents, Sue?' (intention)
SUE: 'I (copy)**²** them.' (intention)
NANCY: 'How (do)**³** it?' (intention)
SUE: 'On the copier.'
NANCY: 'It (be)**⁴** cheaper, if you (make)**⁵** a stencil.' (conditional)
SUE: 'It (take)**⁶** longer, if I (type)**⁷** a stencil, and the manager asked me (finish)**⁸** this work quickly.' (conditional and reported speech).
NANCY: 'Well, Jane (use)**⁹** the copier yesterday, and the Managing Director (see)**¹⁰** her and (tell)**¹¹** her that if she (use)**¹²** stencils, she (save)**¹³** a lot of money.' (tenses and conditional)
SUE: 'I agree. If I (do)**¹⁴** that job, I (cut)**¹⁵** a stencil, because there (is)**¹⁶** no hurry, she did not have (complete)**¹⁷** those copies until the end of the week. That (be)**¹⁸** more efficient.' (conditional, tense)
NANCY: 'How many copies she (want)**¹⁹**?' (tense)
SUE: 'A hundred, and if you only (need)**²⁰** a hundred copies, you can (use)**²¹** the spirit duplicator.' (conditional)
NANCY: 'And for thousands of copies they (use)**²²** the offset-litho.'
SUE: 'Yes, but that (be)**²³** in the duplicating room, and it (need)**²⁴** a lot of experience to use it.' (tense)
NANCY: 'You ever (work)**²⁵** with it?' (tense)
SUE: 'I (prepare)**²⁶** work for it, but I (not operate)**²⁷** the machine itself.' (tense)
NANCY: 'What about the thermal copier?'
SUE: 'That (be)**²⁸** very expensive to use. If you (want)**²⁹** to handle that, you must (get)**³⁰** special permission.' (tense and conditional)
NANCY: 'I'd better (go)**³¹** , unless I can (reproduce)**³²** myself in the Accounts Office. They (wonder)**³³** where I am.' (tenses)
SUE: '(Come)**³⁴** along to the copier, I (take)**³⁵** a copy of you and me, (sit)**³⁶** them in our chairs by our desks and we (go)**³⁷** for an early lunch.' (tenses)

Exercise 55

Put the **adverbs** in brackets in their correct positions.
Example: 'Do you work in this department?' (always)
Answer: 'Do you **always** work in this department?'

DAVID: 'Have you worked in the duplicating section?' (ever)**¹**
ELLEN: 'No, I haven't worked there. (ever)**²** But I am using the photocopier on the third floor (always)**³** and I type stencils (sometimes)**⁴**.'
DAVID: 'I have wanted to learn to type stencils (often)**⁵**, but I seem to get the chance (never)**⁶**. I find myself just typing short notes (usually)**⁷**.'
ELLEN: 'Well, you have to be careful typing stencils (generally)**⁸**, as even a small mistake can mean wasting a lot of time correcting it.'
DAVID: 'Do you make mistakes?' (ever)**⁹**
ELLEN: 'I do when I am not concentrating properly (sometimes)**¹⁰**. But there is a pink fluid which you can use to correct them (usually)**¹¹** and you can graft old stencils onto mistakes, then type over the error (generally)**¹²**, but that is a technique I need to use. (seldom)**¹³**
DAVID: 'Why, because the mistakes you make are small ones?' (usually)**¹⁴**
ELLEN: 'No, because when I am not concentrating the mistakes are so big, I have to use a new stencil and retype the piece.'

11.4 Addressing machines

Addressing machines work on the reverse principle to duplicators. Duplicators work from one master to many copies, whereas with an addressing machine many masters are used for many copies.

There are different types of machines which will print from stencils, spirit duplicating copies, or a range of metal and plastic plates.

Stencils are typed on fibres and fixed to frames and can then be 'run off' as an ordinary stencil would be. Plates from **spirit masters** are fitted into plastic frames, and **metal and plastic plates** can work in addressograph machines which stamp addresses onto correspondence through inked ribbons.

There are also **foil masters**, very thin metal plates which can be typed up on typewriters and will then produce impressions on correspondence.

In addition to these methods, computers, and word processors can be programmed to produce addresses.

Exercise 56

The circular letter below which is sent to keep customers informed about the 'Minerva Book Company's' latest plans needs to be brought up to date with the information given.

THE MINERVA BOOK CO PLC

Minerva House
Kings Road
Wallington
Surrey SM6 0AJ

Phone: 01 779 843
Telex: 6918150
Cable: MINERB

Reg: London 61 558J
VAT: 23 657182

To:

Dear

We are pleased to announce that from next April we intend to open our new branch in Tokyo. Our representative Mr. Koichi Oshida will be giving you all the details when he calls on you before the opening.

Our new centre will allow us to expand our present range of technical and educational books and we hope to offer a new series of business and scientific publications translated from English to Japanese.

You will also be pleased to hear that our present trade discount of 25 per cent, and one month credit facilities will still be available, and we hope to cut delivery times from eight weeks to six weeks.

We know our new expansion programme will be welcomed by everyone and hope you will take advantage of our wide range of services.

Yours sincerely,

David Wright
Managing Director

If the letter was set on a floppy disc to use with a word processor, you would simply move the cursor (the indicator on the screen), take out the old information and insert (put in) the updated details. You would also need to put in your customers' addresses and the new date.

The customer's name is Dr. Toshiro Matsui and his address is 6 Nihonbashi 5-chome, Chuo-ku, Tokyo 105.

The date of the letter is 28 March 19 . .

First change: We have opened our new branch in Tokyo at the Minerva Book Centre, Otsuka, 5 chrome, Bunkyo-Ku, Tokyo, the phone number is 638 7710, Telex 3721019 MINSTOR.

Second change: Our representative will have given you details.

Third change: The new series of translated publications has been introduced.

Fourth change: 25% trade discount has now been raised to 33% and delivery is only four weeks not six weeks.

Memorandums

Information in a company can be circulated by face-to-face conversations, staff announcements at meetings, on the internal 'phones, or through written internal circulars called **memorandums**, or **memos**, for short.

These may be posted on staff notice boards for people to read, circulated in 'chain envelopes', which we talked about in unit 8.1, or with a 'circulation slip' (also called a 'routing slip') which is attached to the memo and lists the staff who the memo is for and their department, and as in the case of a chain envelope each person who receives the memo, signs it.

Many companies use different coloured paper for their memorandums to show that the correspondence is internal.

12.1 Layout

A memo may or may not have the company's heading on it, but it will always state who it is from and who it is to, have a date on it, and sometimes a subject heading:

MEMORANDUM
From:
To: 20 July 19 . .
Subject:

Memos are not letters, so there are no opening addresses such as 'Dear Sir/Madam' or 'Dear Mr./Miss/Mrs./Ms. Green, and there are no 'complimentary closures' e.g. yours sincerely/faithfully.

Paragraphs are sometimes numbered as they deal with each point of a subject, particularly if the memo is long – memorandums can be anything from two lines to a couple of pages depending on their content.

12.2 Contents and examples

1 *'What'* Even if the memo has a title, the opening paragraph usually explains *what* the memo is about:
A fire drill will be held . . .
The company is introducing . . .

2 *'Who'* Although the memo is addressed to someone or a group, it should explain *who* will be affected by the information:
This will only affect staff . . .
It is important that *all* staff . . .

THE ROYAL INSURANCE CO. LTD.   MEMORANDUM

On Lok Yuen Building
25 Des Voeux Road
Central
Hong Kong

To: All managers
From: Security Officer
Subject: Security
Date: 19 May 19..

Would all managers please make sure that valuables and confidential information are locked away at all times and that
staff keep their personal belongings with them. The police
have informed us that there has been an increase of 40 per cent
in robberies in this area.
Please inform all the staff in your departments.

P. Lau

P. Lau
Chief Security Officer

Fig. 78 Memorandum: security

MEMORANDUM
THE NATIONAL BANK PLC
Damansara Utama
Petaling Jaya
Selsngor

Tel: 04—53621
Telex: 76191035
Cable: NATBAN

To: All junior staff
From: D. Chu
       Personnel Manager

Subject: Education
Date: 1 September 19..

We have come to an agreement with the local college of further
education for a part-time release scheme for Business Studies

1   The scheme will operate from 1st January 19..

2   Half-day release will only be for approved courses of
     business studies for recognised examinations.

3   The bank will pay for all fees and books on the courses,
     and any examination fees.

4   All junior staff and trainees under the age of nineteen
     years old on that date will be considered, and those
     selected will still be paid their full salary.

5   If you wish to apply for this scheme, see the manager or
     supervisor of your department within the next three weeks
     to discuss the details.

We hope everyone who is concerned will take this opportunity
for further education, which could help them in their career
in banking and commerce.

David Chu

David Chu
Personnel Manager

Fig. 79 Memorandum: educational scheme

3 *'How'* It should also tell people *how* they will be affected:
. . . lunch hours will be interrupted all week because of . . .
This scheme will mean a change in . . .

4 *'When'* It might be necessary to tell those affected *when* the scheme (policy), operation, or change will happen:
As from the beginning of next year, 19 . . . . . .
The new scheme will come into operation on Monday 1 May 19 . . . . .

5 If information is not clear, or the memo is long, and you think it might not be understood, you should encourage the reader(s) to ask someone to explain it:
. . . if you need more details, ask your supervisor or manager
If the scheme causes any problems, please see your manager

Fig. 78 is an example of a short memorandum simply reminding managers to check 'security'.

The memo in fig. 79 is to 'juniors' advising them of an educational scheme the company is running with the local College of Further Education.

The final memo in fig. 80 concerns 'waste' in a company. The memo is not simply an 'order', but explains the reason for the company's policy and makes suggestions as to how the staff can help.

Exercise 57

Answer the questions based on the memo in fig. 79.
1 Can anyone take part in the 'day-release' scheme?
2 What should people do if they want to apply for the scheme?
3 When will the scheme come into operation?
4 What sort of help would the scheme offer people, if they take part in it?
5 Will salaries be affected?
6 Can any subject be studied under the scheme?
7 Who was the memo from?
8 What sort of company was the memo circulated in?

Exercise 58

Answer the questions based on the memo in fig. 80.
1 What suggestion was made to help cut the costs of telexes and cables?
2 How much did power costs increase by in the previous year?
3 Manila envelopes (brown envelopes) can have windows for addresses in them. What three things could be sent using these envelopes?
4 What does the memo say about telephone calls?
5 What should typists do instead of throwing away correspondence with mistakes on it?
6 How much does the memo estimate fibre-tipped pens cost?
7 Does the memo blame any particular department for the previous year's losses.
8 Power should not only be turned off for economic reasons, when not needed, but for another reason; what is it?
9 How can money be saved when sending catalogues, brochures etc?
10 How can stencils be corrected?
11 Who was the memorandum to?
12 How does the company buy its stationery?
13 What happened to sales and profits the previous year?
14 How much did stationery costs rise by?
15 Were the cost increases for copying larger or smaller than the increases in telecommunications' costs?

<u>MEMORANDUM</u>

INTERNATIONAL SUPPLIERS LTD.

To: All personel
From: Mr. Tunji Obitan
       Chief Accountant
Date: 12 November 19..

Ikorudu Road
Ilupeja
Lagos
Nigeria

This memorandum is being circulated to remind everyone that sales
and profits had fallen at the end of the last financial year, and
although there are many reasons for this, you personally can help
by reducing waste in materials and resources.

1   Telecommunications

    Phone calls can only be made for business purposes, and
    international calls should be kept short and to the point.
    Telexes and cables should only be used for urgent communica-
    tions and then written in a brief, but clear, style.
    Our communications' bill increased by 70 per cent last year.

2   Lighting, heating, and power

    All power should be turned off when not being used. Fans,
    heaters, lights, and office machinery should be turned off
    if they are not needed or when you leave the room. Not only
    for economy, but safety as well.
    Last year's power costs increased by over 50 per cent.

3   Stationery and postage

    Stationery is very expensive even when bought in bulk. But
    you can help to reduce costs.
    Do not send out badly produced work, but if it is possible
    to correct small errors with liquid or paper correctors,
    please do so rather than throwing material away.
    Use Manila, window envelopes rather than Bank envelopes for
    invoices, credit notes, debit notes, statements and receipts.
    Remember catalogues, brochures and circulars can be sent by
    second class post if they are not urgent.
    Please use ball point pens, rather than felt tipped pens
    which are five times the cost. Stationery costs rose by 35 per
    cent last year

4   Copies

    Please remember the carbons we buy can be used more than
    fifty times and still give excellent copies.
    Stencils are cheaper than electrostatic copies and should
    be used when possible. Stencils should also be filed care-
    fully so they do not have to be retyped, which wastes time,
    and typing errors can be corrected by correcting fluid or
    grafting, rather than discarding the stencil and beginning
    again.
    Copying costs increased by 45 per cent last year.

We all want International Suppliers to be a successful company
which will mean job security and better conditions for the
staff, therefore your co-operation in these areas will help.

T. Obitan

Tunji Obitan
Chief Accountant

Fig. 80 Memorandum: waste

Exercise 59

Alice and Rick are talking about the 'National Bank's' memo, fig. 79, to let students go on day-release. Choose the correct **infinitive** from the list at the end of the exercise for each of the spaces:

ALICE: 'Have you seen the bank's offer . . .[1] students' go on day-release? They have promised . . .[2] all fees, and are prepared . . .[3] them full salaries, and they say the courses will help staff . . .[4] in their careers. It seems . . .[5] a good opportunity for junior staff who want . . .[6].'

RICK: 'I only looked at the memo quickly, I didn't bother . . .[7] it carefully as I expected . . .[8] at it more carefully later. Do you know how . . .[9] for the course?'

ALICE: 'Yes, the memo told you how . . .[10] information and who . . .[11] . It said you should arrange . . .[12] your department manager.'

RICK: 'Have you seen yours?'

ALICE: 'Yes, I was determined . . .[13] it; and as he happened . . .[14] free that morning I decided . . .[15] an appointment.'

RICK: 'What happened?'

ALICE: 'He told me how . . .[16] the application form and who . . .[17] it to, and where . . .[18] if they offer me an interview.'

RICK: 'Have you completed the application?'

ALICE: 'I decided . . .[19] it straight away, because I mean . . .[20] a B. Tec. course there.'

RICK: 'Well, I think I'll apply . . .[21] there as well.'

ALICE: 'You're too late, Rick. The memo told us . . .[22] our department heads within three weeks, and that was four weeks ago. Next time a memo goes on the notice board, I'll remind you . . .[23] it.'

to be	to give	to let	to pay	to get on	to read	to look	to
see	to enrol	to study	to be	to fill in	to send	to make	to
discuss	to contact	to do	to go	to take	to read	to apply	
to get	to go to	to enrol	to contact				

Exercise 60

The following piece is part of a short talk given by Mr. Obitan, the Chief Accountant, who wrote the memo in fig. 80, on avoiding waste in the company.

Put infinitives, **with** or **without** 'to', in the spaces. There is a list of infinitives to use at the end of the piece.

MR. OBITAN: '. . . and of course we don't intend . . .[1] you . . .[2] one carbon for two hundred letters, you should . . .[3] able . . .[4] these things for yourself. We will let you . . .[5] all the stationery and office facilities you need. And we don't mean . . .[6] staff telephone calls, but you have . . .[7] we are attempting . . .[8] expenses, so you must . . .[9] in any way possible. You ought . . .[10] that if the company's profits are low because people don't bother . . .[11] money where they can or don't understand how . . .[12] then we will all have problems with our salaries and conditions. If anyone happens . . .[13] of ideas, then they are invited . . .[14] their suggestions to their managers. Thank you for listening to me, and if you have any questions, please ask them.'

to put	to help	to cut	to check	to make	to economise	to
think	to judge	to have	to understand	to use	to remember	
to save	to be					

Telecommunications

Telephone calls are charged at **time** and **distance** rates, and in the UK, there are three periods when rates change – cheap rate (Saturday/Sunday and between 16.00 and 08.00 weekdays); standard rate, (Monday to Friday 08.00 to 09.00/1300 to 16.00); peak rate, (Monday to Friday 09.00 to 13.00).

Local calls, in the UK, cover an area of about 900 square miles, and beyond that **trunk call** charges come into operation.

The system of charges are known as subscriber trunk dialling (STD) and this allows home and overseas calls to be made direct or through the operator.

Operator services are added to the cost of the call; however, if you want to make sure you can get the person you want to contact a **person-to-person** call (or personal call) can be arranged, and this can be cheaper for long distance communications. The operator will also arrange for a **transfer charge**, if the person answering agrees, and they will be charged for the call.

Operator connections for wrong numbers are not charged for.

Dialling

Many business and private phones in the UK are being changed from dialling to push button instruments with the more developed functions illustrated in fig. 81.

Tones

In most countries there are different ringing sounds to tell you what is happening to your call. In the UK a **ringing tone** is a double burr. An **engaged tone** is a high whistling sound which is repeated, and **number unobtainable** (which means you cannot get that number) is a continuous high whistle.

If lines outside the local area are engaged, there may be an 'engaged signal' or a recorded voice will tell you to try later. In public phones, where the call is paid for first, a rapid beeping noise tells you to put in your money. On push button boxes, the caller pays first.

There are two types of **switchboards** which link external calls or internal calls – the cord switchboard, which has cables plugged into connections to

Fig. 81 Telephone. This particular British Telecom model has a volume control, to turn up the sound. You can make it automatically dial numbers you use frequently by just pressing 'T' and another key, hold and transfer calls by pressing 'H', and the flashing lights linked to the function buttons will tell you when numbers are busy, ringing or free. (*Courtesy of British Telecom Business Systems*)

make contacts, and key switchboards, which work in the same way but use 'keys' instead of cords.

These are known as Private Manual Branch Exchange switchboards, or PMBX for short, and they are rented from the telecommunications company.

Large switchboards need operators to run them, but in a small company a number of the staff may handle the switchboard if the operator or receptionist is not there. There are also Private Automatic Branch Exchanges (PABX) which allow staff to dial internal and external calls themselves, the operator only being used for incoming calls.

Some switchboards with microchip circuits will 'stack calls' or divert them when the switchboard is very busy.

Internal office phone equipment

In fig. 81 we saw that the phone has developed into a small computer extension which can store and dial numbers, stack calls, offer an answering service facility and flash signals to indicate incoming calls, engaged lines, and phone ringing.

British Telecom along with other companies offer a wide range of separate equipment that handle these functions separately. From tape recorder **answering machines** that will tell the caller you are out, and take a message, to **punched card callmakers**, which operate by placing a card into a unit, to **taped callmakers**, which make calls by using magnetic tapes with numbers already entered on them, and the caller simply moves the tape along to the number they want, press a button and the phone will do the rest.

Telecommunications services

Among the services offered by the Telecommunication's company are **personal calls** and **transfer charges, alarm calls** (getting you up at a certain time), **directory enquiries** for phone numbers, and **timed calls** (where the operator times the call).

Phone cards, which are bought from the Post Office, are now widely used instead of money. This card gives a credited number of calls on a plastic card and is put into public phones just as money is.

Credit cards are also available and callers give their card number to the operator, who will connect them. The callers are later billed for their calls.

Telemessages in the UK have replaced 'telegrams' but are simply telegrams sent through the operator and can be used for 'congratulations' or 'best wishes' style of telegrams.

Exercise 61

Put the correct **preposition** into the spaces in this extract.
British Telecom ——^{1} ——^{2} other companies offer a wide range ——^{3} equipment ——^{4} tape recorder answering machines, ——^{5} punched card callmakers, which operate ——^{6} placing a card ——^{7} a unit, ——^{8} taped callmakers, which make calls ——^{9} using magnetic tapes ——^{10} numbers entered ——^{11} them. The caller simply moves the tape ——^{12} ——^{13} the number they want, press a button ——^{14} the machine, and the phone will do the rest ——^{15} the work ——^{16} them.

Exercise 62

We saw in unit 13, exercise 16, that certain words take **gerunds** and in unit 12, exercise 59, that other words take **infinitives**.

Put the gerund or infinitive in place of the words in brackets:

Example: 'I'm thinking about (go) to Lagos because I want (work) in a large city.'

Answer: 'I'm thinking about **going** to Lagos because I want **to work** in a large city.'

NMAKO: 'I was thinking of (contact)^1 my family in Lagos.'
FRANCES: 'How do'you want (contact)^2 them? Are you planning (phone)^3 or (write)^4 to them?'
NMAKO: 'I considered (write)^5 but it's not worth (do)^6 that as it takes too long, and I promised (get)^7 in touch with them and let them (know)^8 what it is like (live)^9 here.'
FRANCES: 'I hate (phone)^{10} long distances, I don't enjoy (spend)^{11} all that money, when I can (say)^{12} the same things in a letter.'
NMAKO: 'Well, I wouldn't dream of (use)^{13} the operator (put)^{14} me through I use the STD system and dial myself.'
FRANCES: 'But if the person you wanted, wasn't there, you would have (keep)^{15} (put)^{16} money in.'
NMAKO: 'No, I'll try (get)^{17} a transfer call, so my mother will pay.'
FRANCES: 'Doesn't she mind (pay)^{18} for your calls?'
NMAKO: 'Well, she asked me (contact)^{19} her and while she might persuade me (call)^{20} her regularly, she won't convince me (pay)^{21} for (call)^{22} her regularly!'

Exercise 63

What would you do? What would you say?
Choose the correct answer, from the three given, on these questions concerning telephone techniques.
1 When answering the phone, do you (a) say 'hallo' and give your name, (b) give

the name of your firm and the number, (c) ask who is speaking?

2   If a caller has come through to the wrong department, would you (a) tell them you will contact the switchboard who will put them through to the right department, (b) ask them to redial the correct number themselves, (c) go up three floors to get the person they want to talk to?

3   If you answer the phone for your manager and he indicates that he does not want to speak to the caller, would you (a) say he is in but does not want to speak to them, (b) say he is out, (c) say he is out, but you could take a message?

4   If you were in the UK answering an office phone and heard rapid 'pips', would you think the call was (a) external, (b) internal, (c) an overseas call?

5   If you were asked to make a 'reverse charges' call, what would you say to the operator (a) I want to make a 'person-to-person' call, (b) I want a special service, (c) I want to make a transfer charge call.

6   If you knew you could not contact the person the caller wants for the next half hour, would you (a) apologise, explain the situation and ask them to call back, (b) just ask them to call back, (c) ask them to hold on?

7   If you took a call on reception and the caller said they preferred to hold on for the person they wanted to speak to, would you then (a) leave them until that person arrived to take the call, (b) let them know what is happening every few minutes, (c) insist that they call back later?

8   If you have to take a message for someone, would you (a) find any piece of paper handy and write on it, (b) ask a caller to wait a moment and find a proper note pad, (c) say you cannot take a message as you do not have any paper at present?

9   If you are taking a message, would you say, (a) 'could I have your name and phone number, please', then get all the details, (b) 'give me the details', (c) 'what's your name and number.'

10   If someone comes through to the wrong department and you answer the phone, would you (a) listen patiently while they explain their business, no matter how long it takes, (b) hang up, (c) interrupt them, as soon as you realise their mistake, and tell them you will transfer them?

13.3 Other services

Emergency services

All countries usually have a single number for emergency services – in the UK it is 999. The operator answers and will ask 'which service do you require?' There is no need to explain the problem, simply state whether it is Fire, Police, Ambulance, or rescue services, and you will be put through. Give the service your name, number, address you are calling from, and then explain the details, slowly and carefully, so that the right service will go to the right place, with the right equipment.

If the emergency concerns power problems, without fire dangers, such as gas, electricity or water, phone the company concerned, their number will be in the directory. If it is a medical problem which needs a doctor rather than an ambulance, call a local doctor's number and explain the problem, do *not* dial emergency services in these cases.

Datel

In Europe, the USA, and a number of other countries the **data transmission**

service, Datel, is available, for firms' computers to link up with overseas computers and terminal by phone. Data, information, can be received or sent, processed, and printed out using this service, which simply requires the caller to 'dial' the code of the computer.

Prestel

A home television set and phone linked to the 'Prestel' system allows users to simply dial the service and the type of information they want and it will appear on their TV screens which will act as a VDU. This is one of the **viewdata** services we look at in Unit 10.4.

Confravision

The telecommunications companies in many countries can offer a service which links groups of people in different parts of the country by television so they can hold conferences. In the UK this is called **Confravision**.

Times the conferences are to be held are booked with the telecommunications network and studios are arranged for the link up. International conferences can also be arranged, one of the most important being held in 1984 between Russian and American nuclear scientists on the after-effects of atomic war with both countries linked through a Confravision system.

Teleprinters

These machines have developed from 'ticker-tape' machines which give information on a continuous tape. Stock markets and newspaper offices are only two of the users of teleprinters. However, with communications development the teleprinter is being replaced by more complicated machines which include computer, television, and telephone connections which not only give huge amounts of information, but will analyse (work it out) it as well.

Facsimile communication (Fax)

These machines use telephones and copying facilities to send documents, information, drawings, plans or photographs from one place to another in a country, or from country to country. The photo in fig. 82 is an example of a high speed sending (transmitting) and receiving unit.

The machine sends and receives A4/B4 size paper and can reduce B4 sizes to A4 sizes, transmitting (sending) anywhere in the world in 15 seconds. **Input** (putting information in) includes the time, date, page count, department, and the sender's phone numbers which appear on the top of the received copy, as well as the page number.

If the receiver's machine is loaded to accept information, the sender can also transmit copies to an unattended machine if he has the code number of the receiver's machine.

Fig. 82 A facsimile receiver (*Courtesy of British Telecom Business Systems*)

13.4 Telex

A telex is a machine that both sends and receives typed messages as fast as a phone, but with the 'printed' word being a record of what was 'said'.

The machine itself is like a typewriter with the most advanced machines having many word processor functions such as editing, allowing corrections to be made before the message is sent; screens to see incoming and outgoing messages; memories of up to 40 000 characters (about 6700 words) so that messages can be stored on what is called a 'shortcode' (short cut) system, and computer link-ups with data terminals (see Unit 10.4).

The machine in fig. 83 can also send and receive messages without the operator being there if it is programmed.

Using the telex

The operator 'dials' the receiver's number either on a 'dial' like a telephone, or on a keyboard, or can get through by contacting an exchange operator.

Once the number is dialled an **answerback** code will appear on the **teleprinter** telling the sender s/he is through. A wrong answerback code simply means the sender dials again. (Answerback codes can either be in figures, e.g. 7719813, or with letters and figures, e.g. 89014 PT LA D, or figures and words, e.g. 115613 PIMAN).

The operator then sends his/her answerback code, types the message and repeats the code s/he used.

The receiver's answerback code will appear after the message to show that the message has been received.

Telex codes are found in a **telex directory** which lists users' numbers. There are over 70 000 users in the UK, and nearly one million international telex lines.

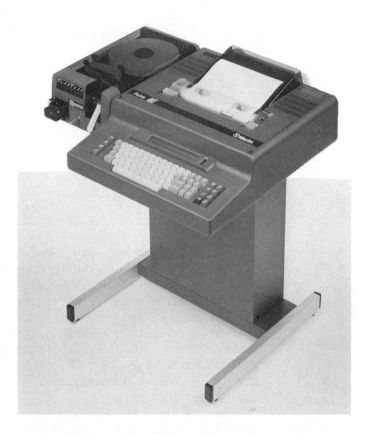

Fig. 83 A telex keyboard and teleprinter (*Courtesy of British Telecom Business Systems*)

Fig. 84 A telex keyboard and display which can also be a VDU screen (*Courtesy of British Telecom Business Systems*)

Layout

```
1  UNISUP

2  915503 BN LT E LONDON

3  WILL INCREASE TRADE DISCOUNT TO 35 0/0 IF ORDER MORE THAN
   2000 UNITS CFM

4  915503 BN LT E LONDON

5  35 0/0 MORE THEN 2000 + ?

6  UNISUP
```

1 Answerback code from receiver (called the **correspondent**), in this case it is an abbreviated name for **Uni**versal **Sup**pliers = UNISUP.
2 Sender's answerback code.
3 Message in cablese, which is cable language using abbreviations where possible, but making sure the receiver will **understand** the message.

　　Telexes are charged by distance and time used, just as long distance phone calls are, so brief messages are necessary. There is a way of cutting language use down for cables and telexes and there is an international code of abbreviations used for telex. We will look at both after this section.

　　Notice that in this message 35 per cent is written 35 0/0 this is because some telexes do not have % signs, so zero, stroke, zero is used, e.g. 0/0.

　　CFM is also an abbreviation for 'please confirm' or confirm that this offer is acceptable.
4 The sender's code is repeated. Notice this code happens to be figures and letters, not a 'contraction' of two words like Universal Suppliers (UNISUP).
5 **Collation** – the main points of a message might be repeated to make sure the receiver understands, this is called **collation** and here, 35% and more than 2000 units are repeated. The plus and question mark sign (+ ?) means **reply, confirm**, or a further message will be sent.

　　When the sign at the end of the message is + it means the end of the message is not clear (the receiver does not understand the previous message). If the sign is + +, it means this is the **final** message.
6 This is the receiver's code (the correspondent's code) to show s/he has received the message.

Further points

Corrections in words are made by typing five Xs, e.g. WE RECIEXXXXX REECXXXXX RECEIVED YOUR MESSAGE YESTERDAY, or E space E space E, e.g. WE RECEIEE E E WE RECEIVED YOUR MESSAGE YESTERDAY.

The **Upper Case** (capital letters) are used to send telexes, and sometimes telex keyboards do not have **fractions**, e.g. ½, ⅓, ¼ or percentages %, or certain **symbols**, e.g. £, $, @ etc.

Fractions can be typed 1/2 (½), 1/3 (⅓), or 1/4 (¼), and **percentages** 0/0 (%) or written PER CENT. Symbols can be written in words, e.g. SIX THOUSAND AMERICAN DOLLARS AT FIVE AND A HALF PERCENT INTEREST PER YEAR, or THREE THOUSAND POUNDS STERLING LOAN FOR TWO AND A HALF MONTHS.

Notice that 'American' or 'US' dollars must be mentioned, as there are Hong Kong and Canadian dollars and Swiss and French Francs etc. 'Pounds sterling' also explained that this referred to the UK **currency**, not **weight**, as in pounds (1 pound = 0.45kg) and ounces (1 ounce = 28.35g).

Language

In some telexes a phrase, a group of words, may be joined as one word for economy, e.g. PLEASE SEND LOWEST ESTIMATE SOONEST = Please send us **your lowest quotations** (prices) as soon as **possible**.

The word 'REPEAT' might be used to make sure the receiver understands the negative, e.g. DO NOT REPEAT NOT SEND CAT NO 561 = Please do **not** send catalogue item number 561.

Certain words can be left out of a message, but **only** if the message still remains clear to the correspondent.

Articles 'the' or 'a' might be left out and **auxiliaries** (*have* received; *can* understand, *will* reply etc.), and the **present participle** might be used (returning) instead of 'are returning'.

Pronouns (him, her, it etc.,) and **possessive pronouns** (yours, our, their) could also be omitted (left out).

We have received **your** order No. 346 **and we are** returning **the** empty cases **as soon as possible**.

In cablese this would become:

RECEIVED ORDER NO 346 RETURNING EMPTY CASES SOONEST

The conjunction (joining word) 'and' was left out in the example, and if there were **prepositions** ('on', 'in', 'under', 'over', 'to', 'for', 'by' etc.), these too might be left out.

We are sending you the information **you wanted by** special delivery service, **and we will** pay **the** costs.

SENDING INFORMATION SPECIAL DELIVERY COSTS PAID

Never sacrifice economy for clarity, in other words, never save money in a cable or telex by not using vital (important) words and losing the sense of the message. It will only cost the company more to make the message clear later, or to repair the damage that might be done if a message is not completely understood:

CHAN DELAYED TAKING LATER FLIGHT

This message is meaningless. What or who is 'Chan', even if we think it refers to a Mr. Chan, why was he delayed and where was he coming or going to? If he was coming to our company, when will he take the next flight? What is its number? Where will it arrive? Does somebody have to meet him, or *her*?

IF the reply was just as brief (short) it would only create more confusion:
TELEX NOT CLEAR REPEAT

Which telex was not clear? Does 'clear repeat' mean 'the telex was not a *clear repeat*' of one we sent? Or does it mean you repeat your message?

If you are not sure that the message will be completely understood, then write it out in full:
WE DID NOT UNDERSTAND YOUR TELEX PLEASE REPEAT IT

Abbreviations

There are internationally recognised abbreviations for telexing, and a Post Office reference book, or the booklet given to your company when it buys or rents their telex will give them a list. Here are some of the main abbreviations:

ABS	Absent subscriber office closed
BK	I have cut off (I stopped sending the telex)
CFM	Confirm, please confim (please acknowledge)
COL	Collation please; I collate; (repeat the important part of the telex again)
CRV	Do you receive well? I receive well
DER	Out of order (telex not working)
DF	You are in communication with the subscriber you called
EEE	I have made an error
FIN	My message(s) is/are finished
GA	You may transmit; can I transmit
INF	Subscriber temporarily unobtainable, call information or enquiry service
MNS	Minutes
MOM	Please wait; I am waiting
MUT	Mutilated – the telex cannot be understood – the telex I sent was badly produced
NA	Correspondence to this subscriber is not allowed
NC	No circuits
NCH	Subscriber's number has been changed (look at a Telex directory for the new number, or get it through the exchange).
NP	Your correspondent is not or is no longer a subscriber.
NR	Tell me your call number; my call number is . . .
OCC	Engaged (try again later)
OK	I agree; do you agree?
P*	(or figure 0) Stop your transmission (stop sending)
PPR	Paper
R	Received
RAP	I will call you back
RPT	Please repeat; or I will repeat
SVP	Please
TAX	What is the charge? or The charge is . . .
TEST MSG	Please send a test message
THRU	You are communicating with a telex (you are through)
TPR	Teleprinter

W   Words
WRU   Who is there?
XXXXX   A mistake has been made
*   Repeat until transmission is stopped

Exercise 64

Compose the three following telexes from the information given:

(i) Your company's answerback code is 6918150, which stands for Minerva Booksellers Ltd. and your customer is the Tokyo Book Centre, Telex 881091.

Tell them that you have received their order No. 573, but you cannot get 'Business Writing' catalogue No. 34, as it is being reprinted. However, you do have 'Business Communications' catalogue No. A17 which you can include in their order. Use the sign asking for their confirmation in their reply.

(ii) Send a telex for Business Machines PLC, answerback BUSMAC to The Nigerian Insurance Company Ltd., Telex answerback 716813 Lagos, telling them that the IBX computer they enquired about will cost $5321.00 US, however, there will be a 15 per cent trade discount off the price. Use the sign to show that is the end of your message.

(iii) Telex 'Menswear Fashions Ltd.' London, answerback 791013 London, from your company, HK Manufacturers Ltd. Telex HOKMAN 610561 and explain there will be a delay on their order, Invoice No. C1980, of six weeks because of a fire in your factory. Say you are sorry, but the delay is unavoidable, however, you can guarantee delivery six weeks from the promised date.

What are the three following telexes saying? Notice any inclusions and say what they mean:

(iv)   This is a reply from the Tokyo Book Centre in (i)
        6918150
        881091
        ACCEPT 25 COYS BUS COM CAT NO A17 INCULXXXXX INUCXXXXX
        INCLUDE IN ORDER NO 45 CNM TDE DISC 33 0/0 REPEAT 33 0/0
        881091
        33 0/0 + ?

(v)   Confirming an arrival
        571681 LONDON
        901315 BL MO S
        MR CHAN SLS MNGR ARRIVING 20 MAY HTHROW ETA. 08.30 CFM
        BOOKING 6 DAY BOOKING IN ROYAL HOTEL AND REP TO MEET HIM
        + ?
        901315 BL MO S
        571681 LONDON

(vi)   Reply to (ii)
        BUSMAC
        716813 LAGOS
        ACCEPT QUOTE IBX FOUR THOUSAND FIVE HUNDRED AND TWENTY
        ONE US DOLLARS NET IF YOU CAN DELIVER WITHIN EIGHT WEEKS
        OR SOONEST OFFICIAL ORDER FOLLOWS CFM
        716813 LAGOS
        4521 DOLLARS US NET + ?
        BUSMAC

Exercise 65

What do the following abbreviations mean, check your answers with the list on page 134.

ABS	DER	FIN	MNS	NCH	OCC	OK
P*	R	RPT	TAX	XXXXX	THRU	E E E

Exercise 66

Here are some instructions on using a telex. Choose the correct **infinitives** from the list below.

The first thing ———[1] when using the telex is that it is like a phone.

If you know how ———[2] a phone and how ———[3] the machine is quite simple. Your first job is ———[4] the number you want, and your second task is ———[5] until your correspondent's answerback code appears. The third thing ———[6] is use your own answerback code, not only ———[7] your correspondent know who they are talking to, but ———[8] them a reference ———[9] themselves.

It is best ———[10] the telex short unless you want ———[11] a lot of money, because like a long distance call, telexes are only used ———[12] fast contact with people. Once the two answerback codes appear, you can ———[13] your message.

to type   to do   to let   to contact   to make   to use   to give   to send   wait   to remember   to dial   to keep   to spend

Exercise 67

Put the words in brackets into the **infinitive** to shorten the sentences in this piece.

Example: 'She went to London (so that she could find a job).'
Answer: 'She went to London **to find** a job.'

We use telexes (so that we can get in touch)[1] with people more quickly. But we write in cabelese – cable language – (so that we can make)[2] the messages shorter. You would be sorry (if you found out)[3] that the telex you sent (when you wanted to save money)[4] was as much as the journey to the correspondent would have cost. (In order that we make)[5] ourselves clear, we repeat words and phrases (so that we can stress)[6] the important parts of the message. Our clients would be annoyed (if they received)[7] messages that they could not understand because the important point had not been made clearly. Therefore, operators, (who want to cut costs)[8], always remember (that they should send)[9] brief but clear telexes and (that just by saving)[10] a little money, they might lose the meaning of the message.

Tables, charts and graphs

Tables are lists of figures which give explanations. The **time-table** you used at school was a list of classes you had to go to and the hours you should have been in them.

Travel **time-tables** explain when buses, trains, ships, and planes leave and arrive. These sorts of time-tables are usually read across, from left to right. When tables give totals at the beginning and foot of columns they are read across and up and down, like the Petty Cash Analysis in fig. 48, page 83.

Some tables are used for interpretation (translation), as in fig. 85, which interprets Arabic numerals (numbers), which are used in most countries, into Roman numerals, which are still used to give dates and classifications (categories).

1	2	3	4	5	6	7	8	9	10
I	II	III	IV	V	VI	VII	VIII	IX	X
11	12	13	14	15	16	17	18	19	20
XI	XII	XIII	IXV	XV	XVI	XVII	XVIII	XIX	XX
25	30	35	40	45	50	55	60	65	70
XXV	XXX	XXXV	XL	XLV	L	LV	LX	LXV	LXX
75	80	90	100	200	300	400	500	600	700
LXXV	LXXX	XC	C	CC	CCC	CD	D	DC	DCC
800	900	1000	2000						
DCCC	CM	M	MM						

Fig. 85 Table of Roman and Arabic numerals.
Table information: There are seven letters representing figures in Roman numerals: I, one; V, five; X, ten; L, fifty, C, one hundred; D, five hundred; M one thousand. If there are two letters and the first is lower than the second in value, e.g. IV, or IX, then deduct the first from the second to get the Arabic figure: IX = X(10) − I(1) = 9; IV = V(5) − I(1) = 4.

Tables are used to give you quick information and might just be headed (with titles) with boxes saying 'yes' or 'no' to indicate whether a product does or does not have certain advantages, or accessories (other products to use with it).

Figure 86 is a table explaining which accessories are included in the prices of different models of the same car:

Model	Sun Roof	Radio**	Cassette**	Gears	Speed m.p.h.	Petrol Consumption*	Cigar Lighter	Elect. Windows
De Luxe	Yes	Yes	Yes	5	130	28	Yes	Yes
LS 1500	Yes	Yes	Yes	5	100	28	Yes	No
LS 1200	No	Yes	No	4	90	40	No	No
LS 1100	No	No	No	4	80	45	No	No
LS 850	No	No	No	4	80	50	No	No

*Petrol consumption in town driving at 40 m.p.h. in miles per gallon.
**Can be included as extras.

Fig. 86 Table explaining the accessories of different models of a car

The important thing to remember about tables, is that they are not there to confuse you, as they might seem to do when you first look at all the figures and details. They are made so that people can see 'at a glance' (a quick look) the details of a product, or figures of accounts. To write all that information given in fig. 86, would probably take two or three pages.

Finally, here is a table for four shops which belong to the same company giving their 'turnovers' (the amount of money they made) for each group of articles they sold in a week, per shop, and for the group, and the total turnover for each shop (not each item) and the group, as a whole, for the week, fig. 87.

HIS AND HERS CLOTHING LTD Sales Table for the week ending March 18, 19 . .								
Branch	Jeans $	Shirts $	Sweaters $	Jackets $	Coats $	Skirts $	Hosiery $	Total $
Dean St.	700.00	340.20	132.52	400.00	900.00	250.54	n.a.	2723.26
Base Rd.	631.20	351.19	169.10	251.00	600.00	n.a.	30.00	2032.49
Druse St.	510.25	158.13	170.00	360.00	411.00	274.41	45.15	1928.94
Dock Est.	1351.17	753.17	256.25	1795.00	2147.00	685.65	98.16	7086.40
Total	3192.62	1602.69	727.87	2806.00	4058.00	1210.60	174.11	13771.09

n.a. not applicable

Fig. 87 Sales table for shop branches

By looking at the table in fig. 87, we can see that the Dock Estate branch has done much better than the other branches ($7086.40) and that the Druse Street branch does not do as well as the other branches. And by a quick check we can find out which shop does better at selling one line of clothes rather than another, for example, although Base Street has a better turnover in coats than Druse Street, it does not do as well in jackets. But to get a really accurate (precise) picture, we would also have to know the quantity of garments, e.g. how many units of each line do the shops sell, as this table simply gives us amounts in dollars, not units and dollars. So although Base Street earns more money in coats than Druse Street, this might simply be because their prices are higher, as they may sell a better quality of coat.

Notice, also, that the abbreviation 'n.a.' appears in the table. In this case it means **not applicable** – does not apply – to this branch, perhaps because the branch does not sell that line. But 'n.a.' also can mean **not available**, in say, government tables, where the government either will not give the figures, or they have not yet worked them out.

Exercise 68

These questions are based on the tables in this unit.

Fig. 86

1 Do you get a radio with the LS 1200 model?
2 What is the petrol consumption in town driving for the LS 850?
3 Which model(s) are the most expensive to run?
4 Which model(s) are the least expensive to run?
5 Which is the fastest model?

Fig. 87

6 Which shop had the lowest turnover that week?
7 Which shop does not sell skirts?
8 Which shop has the best turnover in jeans?
9 Which shop had the worst turnover in sweaters?
10 What was the total turnover in jackets for that week?

Fig. 85

11 If a film was made in MCMLXXX, in which year would it have been made?
12 If you saw a statue which was put up in MDCCC, when would it have been erected?
13 If a box of metal parts was numbered No. VII, how many other boxes would you think there would be, if that was the last one?
14 If both hands of a classic faced watch were pointing to XII, what would the time be?
15 Some people use roman numerals for months of the year, which month would VI represent?

14.2 Charts and graphs

The words **chart** and **graph** are often used in place of one another today without any real difference being made. But if a distinction (difference) were to be made, then a 'chart' is more of an illustration (a drawing) than a graph which is usually made up of lines rather than thick bars, coloured areas, or triangles and squares.

Charts and graphs, like tables of figures, are used to make information and data, easy to read and understandable. **Computer graphics**, computer drawings, can build quite complicated charts, but there is a limit to the amount of information that can be put into any chart before it becomes too complicated.

Bar Charts are produced with **horizontal** bars which are read from left to right, or **vertical** bars, read up and down. The length of the bar gives you an idea of how much or how many are being produced, sold, bought, etc. However, it is essential to remember that in all charts and graphs the units must be uniform; in other words American dollars, or metric weights, or imperial measures (feet and inches) etc., must be compared with one another. You cannot compare, for example, weight and currency, or units of production and measurements.

In fig. 88 there is the Comet Factory's car production for one year from January to December. Notice the months are listed in Roman numerals, I, II, III, IV etc., along the **horizontal axis**, the line going across, and the numbers of cars, the units, are shown on the **vertical axis**, the line going up and down.

The build-up of production to August is because UK car companies produce new car registrations in this month (new number plates) and the biggest demand for cars is during August. And in those months after August production falls as demand falls and Comet's car production workers would be on holiday.

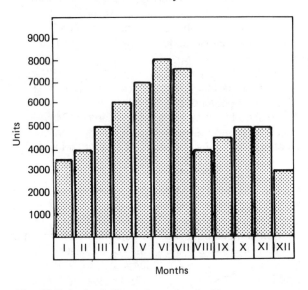

Fig. 88 Bar chart: Comet car production

Bar Charts can be used for comparing units. In fig. 86 we saw that Comet produced five different models. The chart in fig. 89, shows a comparison of **sales** for those five models in the month of August. This time the month is on the vertical axis and the sales are shown horizontally.

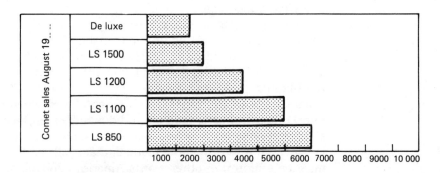

Fig. 89 Bar chart showing August sales for different models

Notice that the de Luxe model, the most expensive in the range, does not sell as well as those lower down the range such as the LS1100 or the LS850, which are cheaper models.

Pie charts, so called because they look like slices of a 'pie' cut up are also produced to give comparisons and information at a glance. They often use percentages for comparisons, but they are limited to the amount of information they can give in one chart. The pie chart in fig. 90 shows the percentage of exports to different areas in the world of the LS 850, one of Comet's models, for a twelve month period.

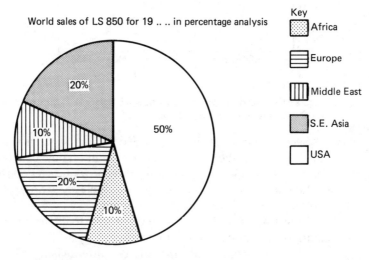

Fig. 90 Pie chart of exports

Pictograms are graphs that use symbols or pictures to give information. They are easy to read as the illustration (the drawings) immediately explain what the figures refer to. Fig. 91 is an insurance company explaining to its

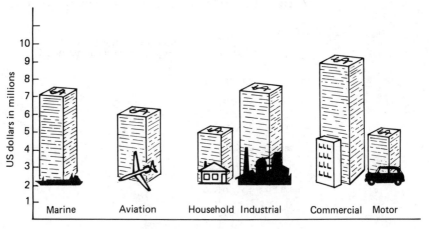

Insurance over for 19 .. .. total $37.5 million

Fig. 91 Pictogram illustrating a company's insurance cover for one year

policyholders (people who insure with them) what the company has insured over the past year. This is really an advertisement to show investors and policyholders how wide the company's interests are.

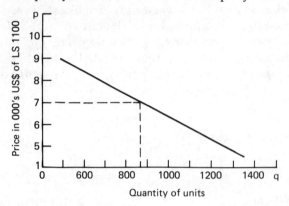

Fig. 92 Demand graph for Comet's LS1100 car. You can see that at 7000 dollars each, Comet can sell 870 cars.

Sector Charts use shapes in the drawings (illustrations) to give the reader an idea of relationships between units. They can use triangles, cubes, circles, rectangles, or squares to show how one section relates to another.

Like most charts there is a 'key' which gives an explanation to what the colours, shaded areas, or designs mean.

Line graphs are lines drawn on graphs to illustrate rises and falls in sales, staff, production, exports, imports etc.

The most familiar graph to many students is the 'demand graph' used in economics. On the vertical axis there is the **price** (p) of the product, and along the horizontal axis the quantity (q) which will be bought at different prices, fig. 92.

In fig. 93 we have a sales graph for twelve months comparing the four branches of His and Hers Clothing Ltd., the company we looked at in fig. 87. The different branches are presented by either dots (. . .), dashes (- - -),

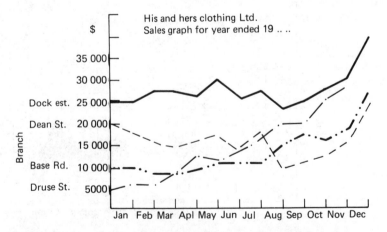

Fig. 93 Line graph comparing sales of different banches

a straight line (―――) or a thicker line. Of course on a wall chart these could be in different colours, with branch names written in the same colour corresponding to their lines.

Charts, graphs and diagrams of any sort must be proportioned (related) properly. If a chart started at $1 million then rose to 1.25 million, and the following year showed 1.50 million it would look like profits of the company or turnover had doubled. Therefore there must be a regular relationship between all the units so they show the 'true position' the chart is demonstrating.

Exercise 69

These exercises are based on the graphs and charts in unit 14.2.

Fig. 88

1 In which month did Comet produce most cars?
2 Why do UK car companies build up production towards August?
3 Which was the month for the lowest production?
4 What was the difference in the number of units produced in February and June?
5 What was the average car production for the last three months of that year?

Fig. 89

6 How many de Luxe models were sold in August?
7 Why were more LS850s sold that month?
8 What was the difference in sales between the LS1500 and LS1100 in that month?

Fig. 90

9 If the total sales for the LS850 were $10 million in the world, how much did the Middle East buy, in dollars?
10 Who was the second biggest importer(s) of LS850s?

Fig. 91

11 How much insurance cover did International offer for shipping in that year?
12 What was the biggest area of insurance cover they offered?

Fig. 92

13 At $8000 a car, how many LS1100s could Comet sell?
14 At what price would Comet only sell 500 LS1100s?

Fig. 93

15 Which branch is represented by a straight line?
16 What was Druse Street's turnover for the month of February?
17 How would you identify Base Road's turnover?
18 Which branch showed the best average turnover that year?

Exercise 70

Choose the correct form of the **adjectives** in the following sentences and put in the articles, 'a'/'the' where necessary.
Example: It is (much, more, most) attractive room in the place
               It is **the most attractive** room in the place
1 (easy, easier, easiest) charts to understand are (simple, simpler, simplest) ones
2 (good, better, best) thing to do when making a graph is to keep it to basics.

(much, more, most) complicated graphs are (less, lesser, least) understood, and even (many, more, most) clear explanations will not make them (easy, easier, easiest) to follow

3 (old, older, oldest) charts in the world are really maps. Yet they can be (much, more, most) beautiful ever produced, even though we have (good, better, best) equipment today than they had in those (early, earlier, earliest) times.

4 Carbon ribbons give (clear, clearer, clearest) type on paper, but cotton ribbons go (far, further, furthest), although they make (less, lesser, least) impression when sending letters to customers. However, electronic machines, which use carbon ribbons, give you (wide, wider, widest) choice in typefaces, so you are not limited to (less, lesser, least) interesting styles of elite and pica. I have even seen an old English typestyle which is (many, more, most) unusual type I have ever known.

5 (much, more, most) useful filing systems are the ones which need (little, less, least) attention except for keeping them in (good, better, best) order and up to date.

Complaints

There are many reasons in commercial life why a complaint might be
necessary.

(i)   The wrong goods may have been sent – you ordered 200 carbon
ribbons, but cotton ribbons were sent instead. You ordered bond
paper, but received bank paper.

(ii)   The goods might have been damaged, sent late, or not delivered at
all. Or your company might keep receiving consignments for
another firm with a similar name, address, or account number.

(iii)   The supplier may have overcharged you.

(iv)   A service, such as a repair, might not have been carried out
properly, so that the engineers have to keep returning to fix the
same machine.

(v)   A customer might not pay his account on time and not reply to
further 'requests' for payment.

Guide to complaining by 'phone

(a)   Check your facts and make absolutely sure it is necessary to
complain – a machine you have may have a set of instructions that
must be followed. If it is not doing its job properly, check that you
followed all the instructions, before you complain about the
machine. If clothes shrink (get small) or fall out of shape after
washing, make sure the instructions had been followed:

The case of the damaged sweater
SUPPLIER: 'Yes, I can see the garment is badly damaged, did you
boil it?
CUSTOMER: 'Er . . . yes.'
SUPPLIER: 'The instructions tell you very clearly 'wool must never
be boiled'. If you look at the label you'll see . . .'

The case of the damaged engine
SUPPLIER: 'I agree, sir, the engine of this car is in a terrible
condition. Do you add water to the radiator?
CUSTOMER: 'Of course I do!'
SUPPLIER: 'When was the last time you did that?'
CUSTOMER: 'When I bought it, four years ago!'
SUPPLIER: 'But didn't you read the manual (book of instructions)
telling you to add water every . . .'

The case of the broken photocopier

ENGINEER: 'I agree the copies are terrible. I suppose you use toner regularly?'

CUSTOMER: 'Toner?'

ENGINEER: 'The black powder that fuses to the paper to give images – you do put toner into the machine, don't you sir?'

CUSTOMER: 'But I thought the machine took photographs like a camera.'

ENGINEER: 'Well this is really a copier and works on a different system. The manual, here, gives you instructions . . .'

(b) Never be rude when complaining, it just creates bad feeling:

CUSTOMER: 'Your company should be put out of business!' (wrong)
'I would like to complain about . . .' (right)

'I have never come across such bad service. This machine has been looked at ten times . . .!' (wrong)
'The engineers do not seem able to fix the machine so I think we'll have to insist on a replacement for it . . .' (right)

'What d'you call this rubbish! I only bought it a couple of days ago, and look at it now!' (wrong)
'This is completely unsatisfactory – the article is new, but look at it now. I must insist on a refund (my money back) or a replacement.' (right)

(c) State the facts clearly so the supplier knows exactly who he is dealing with; which item is causing the problem; what the problem is, and what you want him to do about it.

Customer: 'This is (**name of customer**) of (**address**) and I'm calling about the RX 500 which we bought from you on Invoice No. . . . on (**date**). The machine has a number of faults, first, ... second, ... third, ... Would you send someone to look at it. The best time for him to come would be . . . . .'

Supplier: 'This is (**name of supplier**) of (**address**). We are phoning about the unpaid balance on your July statement for (amount). The account is now four months overdue (late) and we would like to know when it could be cleared. We wrote to you on (**date**) and on (**date**), but did not receive your reply . . .'

(d) Complain immediately, as delays can create problems:

Customer: '. . . I'm complaining about the delivery of (**goods**) which we received yesterday . . .'

Customer: '. . . about the R2000 word processor which was delivered last week. The machine broke down this morning . . .'

(e) Remember your supplier will want to correct mistakes as he wants to keep a good reputation, so have a positive attitude towards him, in other words assume (think) he wants to put things right, and you could even mention (say) that:

Customer: '. . . and I know you would like to help us in this matter . . .'

Customer: '. . . I know your company has an excellent reputation so they will want to help us with this problem.'

(f) Do not always assume (believe) it is your supplier or customer's fault:

Supplier: 'We did not realise that goods were arriving late and are pleased you pointed this out. It could be because of the transport company we're using, and we'll contact them immediately.'

Customer: 'I sent a cheque to you two weeks ago. I can't understand why you haven't received it. I'll make enquiries with our bank and cancel the original cheque.'

(g) If you think you know why or how a problem has happened, it could help to tell your supplier:

Customer: 'Our account number is 4405676 and the invoices we have received have been for 4450676, which seems to show that the figures are being misread (wrongly read).'

Customer: 'Our name is L.A. Smith, of 101 Queens Way, but our parcels are being deliverd to A.L. Smith of 110 Queens Way, do you think you could check this for us?'

Customer: 'We are allowed a *special* quantity discount of 11 per cent, but are only being given the usual 7 per cent. Could you look at a copy of the letter you sent us on 21 June 19 . ., where the special discount was agreed, and if possible note this in your accounting system.'

In a telephone complaint:

(i) Get through to the department you are going to complain to:
'I'd like to speak to . . .' 'Could you connect me with . . .' 'May I speak to . . .'

(ii) State who you are (the name of your company), and address (see example in (c))

(iii) Explain the problem, again, refer to example in (c), and how you want it dealt with.

(iv) Make a note of who you are speaking to, when the call took place, and how the problem was to be settled, and confirm this:
'. . . so, I'm speaking to Mr. Damont in the services department and you will send an engineer to us on Wednesday, 18 March, at 09.30. Good. Will you ask him to ask for Miss Lee, that's me, and I will explain the problem to him? Thank you.'
'So, Mr. Chan . . . I'll just make a note of this, you have sent us a cheque for $5600.45, number 99134 5431 6970, and it was sent on 9th December, and appears to be lost in the post. And you will send us another cheque for that amount, today?'
'Thank you Mr. Chan, I'll give this note to our accountant, who I'm sure will contact you in the next few days to let you know what has happened.'

(v) As in the last example, it is often useful to let the person know you will call back to keep them informed of the situation.

15.2 Letters of complaint

When making a complaint by letter, you can follow the guide given below: Make sure your complaint is justified (right). Do not be rude. State your facts clearly; complain as soon as possible; assume your supplier wants to help you, and that the problem might not have been caused by him; offer any information that will help with a solution. It is also very useful to find out, before you write your letter, who to contact in the company, as personal correspondence makes things happen more quickly.

(a) Openings
I am writing to complain about the . . .
This letter concerns the (**name of product**) which we bought from you on . . . , invoice no. . . .
I would like to complain about . . .

(b) Details
Since we first got the machine we have had problems with the/there have been a number of problems with . . .
Goods have been delivered later than our agreement. Order Nos. 371, 563, 960, for example, were delivered two weeks later than scheduled (planned) . . .
The main problem appears to be . . .

(c) Suggestions
We think the mistake could have been caused by . . .
It is possible that the fault is in the construction/casing/machinery etc.
It appears that the problem is due to (because of) . . .

(d) Action
Would you please look into this as soon as possible.
It is very important that this fault/mistake/error is corrected as soon as possible . . .
We would like this dealt with within the next week.

(e) Close
We look forward to hearing from you within the next few days.
Please contact us to let us know when your service engineers will be coming.
We look forward to receiving the replacement within the next two weeks.

Here is a full letter of complaint:

STATIONERY SUPPLIERS LTD

63 Rathbone Place
London W1A 1AA

Tel- 01-678 9100
Telex- 8910153

Sales Manager   8 May 19..
The International Paper Co.
Gamla Brogatan 59
10121 Stockholm
Sweden

Dear Mr. Olsen,

We are writing to complain about your last shipment of
A4 and A5 paper, Order No. C5617, which we received
yesterday.

Most of the packets were damaged, with the paper being
crushed and stained as though the parcels had been roughly
handled.

We know this might have happened while the goods were being
transported, and if this is so, we advise you to contact
your shippers. However, as we cannot sell the paper, would
you please send a replacement for the whole order, as we
ourselves have customers for this stationery, and let us
know whether you want us to return the damaged consignment
carriage forward, or keep it for inspection.

We look forward to receiving the replacement within the
next few days.

Yours sincerely,

L. Marks

L. Marks
Buying Manager

Notice how Mr. Marks in his letter explains the damage to the goods in detail, but does not 'assume' his supplier is responsible, and how he explains how he wants the problem solved, by receiving a replacement order, carriage forward (which means the supplier will pay postage). Finally, he wants to know what should be done with the damaged goods.

Here is another example of a personal complaint:

```
                                         48 King's Road
                                         Hong Kong

The Manager                              4 April 19..
D.D. Electrics
Yik Yin Building
To Kwan Road
Kowloon


Dear Sir,

I am writing to complain about your 'Electrocolor
Television', which I bought from you on 2 March 19..,
Invoice No EM 67103.

Since I have had the set, I have had to call your
service engineers four times to see to both the sound
and vision of the set as it is sometimes impossible to
get either clear sound or picture.

The television is guaranteed for one year, but I do not
intend to keep calling engineers who can only repair the
set temporarily.

Would you please either replace the television with a
new one, or give me a refund.

I have always found your products to be satisfactory, so
I am sure a company with your reputation will fulfil its
guarantees to their consumers.

I hope to hear from you within the next few weeks.


Yours faithfully,

Chi Wai Law

Chi Wai Law (Mrs.)
```

15.3 The language of complaints

The language of complaint, whether it is on the phone or written should be impersonal (trying to avoid expressions like 'your mistake', 'your fault', 'your bad service'). Using the definite article can avoid this – '**the** mistake', '**the** fault', '**the** bad service'.

The passive voice can also stop the complaint sounding 'accusing' (guilty) or unpleasant:

You sent the delivery late – (passive) The delivery **was sent** late.
You must clear your account – (passive) The account **must be cleared**.

We want you to replace the damaged goods – (passive) We would like the damaged goods **to be replaced**.

Try not to give *orders*:

You must exchange this . . . – We would like you to exchange . . .
You have to send us . . . – Could you/Would you send us . . .
We want . . . – We would prefer/would like . . .
Do not post fragile goods . . . – It would be better if you did not post fragile (breakable) goods . . .

Do not use 'shock' words:

We were shocked/amazed . . . – We were surprised . . .
We were disgusted . . . – We were not happy with . . .
We could not believe that you would sell . . . – We were disappointed to find that you sell . . .
I have never before known a company to produce goods like this Garbage/rubbish/trash – It is unusual for a company to produce goods like this, which are unsatisfactory/unsuitable

Exercise 71

Reword the following sentences to make them more acceptable:
1 You must pay your outstanding balance in our account.
2 We were disgusted when we received the product and could not for the life of us believe you'd sell such rubbish.
3 Don't send valuables by ordinary post, register them!
4 In ten years of trading I've never known a company to sell such rubbish.
5 When I opened the container, I thought my god, what the hell is this!
6 We were shocked to find you hadn't sent a cheque.
7 I want the manager fast, because I want to give him hell over this faulty machine.
8 It's your fault, not our fault, that delivery was delayed, because you did not complete the delivery note properly.

Exercise 72

Put the correct words, from the list below, into this letter complaining to a supplier that this is the fourth time he has delivered the wrong consignment (parcel of goods) to your company.

Dear Mr. Errol,

I am writing to you ———**1** wrong ———**2**.
Over the past three months we have had four ———**3** wrongly delivered to our company and this has caused ———**4** in delivering to our own ———**5**, as we have had to wait up to ten days before the ———**6** consignment is sent to us.
Would you please make sure in ———**7** that our ———**8** are clearly ———**9** and your drivers are instructed to double ———**10** their addresses so that these ———**11** do not occur again.
Unless we can ———**12** on you in future, I am sorry to say that we will have to find an alternative ———**13**.

Yours sincerely,

J. Thompson
Purchasing Director.

rely   parcels   consignments   marked   concerning   future
customers   supplier   mistakes   correct   delays   deliveries
check

15.4 Dealing with complaints

Here is a guide to handling customers' complaints on the phone.

(a) Assume your customer's complaint is genuine (honest) and that h/she is not trying to get better terms, e.g. a discount, or is complaining without any good reason. Therefore, be helpful, not only with the words you use, but the way you speak:

'Oh . . . that is unusual for this model'

'The salesman was rude to you . . . well, that's surprising . . .'

'Deliveries are always late . . . well that certainly is a reason to complain and needs checking . . .'

'The tee shirts shrunk (got smaller) as soon as they were washed? That is unusual . . . I wonder if you could tell me how you washed them?'

'. . . and you say the machine broke . . . could you let me know exactly how you used it?'

Remember, your company has probably spent a lot of money advertising their goods and services. This money would be wasted if their staff try to save a few pounds or dollars by rejecting a complaint without considering the customer's views carefully.

(b) Make a note of all the customer's details, name, address, and the details of the item:

'Can I have your name and address please . . . good. Can you give me the name and number (if there is one) of the machine?'

'. . . good, I've got your name and address, now can you give me the catalogue number of the item?'

'. . . I've written your name and address, now is it possible for you to give me the Order number and Invoice number of the . . .'

Get the exact details of the complaint. A note to your manager or the service department saying 'the machine doesn't work', or 'the customer complained about our delivery service', is not enough information:

'. . . now, Mrs. Grey, can you tell me exactly what is wrong with the washing machine . . . I'll just make a note "it leaks (spills water) whenever you use it" . . . and this has happened before.'

'. . . you say that on the 5th July, 8th August, and 19th September order numbers 671, 903, and 1005, were delivered ten days late and the driver could not give you any explanation . . .'

'. . . yes, I've your name and address . . . now, the whole batch (group) of pens we supplied did not work at all although they did have ink in them, and you tried warming them to let the ink flow (run)?'

Get details of what the customer would like you to do. Do they want **repairs** – if they do, when would it be convenient (the best time) to call? Do they want **replacements** (another item in place of the one they have), or do they want a **refund** (their money back) or a **credit**

note (a note crediting them with the amount of money the item cost)?

You will probably not be able to make the decision about replacements or refunds, and you should tell the customer this *clearly*. But it is useful for your manager to know what the customer expects:

'Well, I certainly can't make any decisions, but would you like our engineers to call and look at the machine?'

'It's not possible for me to make a decision, but could you let me know what you would like us to do?'

'. . . now, would you like me to make a note that you would like a credit note, rather than a replacement? Of course that will be passed on to our department manager, and he will contact you.'

'I can't tell you whether you are entitled (have the right) to a replacement. But I can make a note saying that that is what you've asked for.'

(c)   Customers can be angry when they complain, so be **sympathetic** (understanding), listen to them patiently, never raise your voice or get into an argument. Never agree that your company's products are faulty, quite the opposite, stress (press) that complaints are unusual, but at the same time, be **understanding**, but never make a promise that cannot be kept.

'. . . really, is that what happened? That must've been unpleasant for you . . .' (Customer: 'Your company's machines are useless'). 'I can't agree with that. We export all over the world, and I can't remember a complaint about this model; however, from what you say, this does need looking into . . .'

'. . . oh, I can see how that can be inconvenient . . . and yes, I agree it shouldn't have happened, that's why I'm going to pass this message along to my supervisor immediately and she'll deal with it right away, I'm sure.'

'. . . well that sounds like you have a problem with the battery, but you'll need our service engineers to look at it before any decision can be made . . . (Customer: 'What a waste of time!') 'Yes, these things do take time, but that's really the only way we can deal with it . . . (Customer: 'Your company isn't much use is it!') 'I think you'll find any company would have to at least look at the machine before they can decide on what can be done.'

(d)   Never blame any of the staff for faults in goods or services.

(e)   Always *thank* the customer, whether s/he is right or wrong, for bringing the complaint to your attention (making you aware of it). And tell them your company is always there to assist them:

'Well, thank you very much for telling us about this, and we'll certainly look into it.'

'Thank you for calling and letting us know, and we'll get right on to it (deal with it) immediately.'

'We appreciate you calling us. We're always interested in our customers' views, and we'll certainly send an engineer to inspect the machine.'

(f)   You should not leave anyone 'hanging on' the phone, particularly an angry customer. If you have to, explain you will be away for a moment, and what you will be doing, then get back as soon as you can.

'I'm sorry, I must check your invoice and order number, could you just hold on for a moment, or would you prefer me to phone you back?'

'Could you just hold on for a second while I get a pen and paper, this isn't my extension number . . .' (Customer: No, I can't!) 'Well would you like me to call you back' (meanwhile indicate to someone else in the office that you need a pen and paper now!)

'If you can just give me a moment, I'll take all the details.'

15.5 Writing an answer to complaints

(a)   Thank the customer for writing to you and refer to the date of his/her letter and the complaint, and deal with it immediately:

Thank you for writing to us on 5th November concerning the problems you have with the XG 100.

Thank you for your letter of 8th May explaining the difficulties you have had with deliveries.

(b)   Deal with the complaint sympathetically:

I was sorry to hear that you have had difficulty with . . . and I can assure you that this is unusual. However, we are instructing our service department to send an engineer to you within the next few days, and they will contact you to make an appointment.

We were surprised to hear that our deliveries to you on (**dates**) for (**invoice and order numbers**) were overdue by ten days, and we will look into this immediately.

(c)   Once a complaint has been looked into (examined) then reply explaining the situation.

(i)   Dear Mr. ....

Our technicians have now examined the batch of faulty pens you complained about in your letter of (date).

They found the ink used was of a substandard (low standard) quality and we apologise for the inconvenience this has caused. We can either send you a new batch as per the sample enclosed, carriage paid, or a credit note for (amount). If you accept the new batch, we will offer you a 10 per cent discount off the list prices for the inconvenience, or alternatively 10 per cent off your next order.

Thank you for drawing our attention to this fault.

Yours sincerely,

Notice the letter accepts the customer's complaint; explains what was done about it; apologises for the inconvenience (trouble) caused; gives two alternatives (a new supply or credit note); offers a discount and thanks the customer for complaining.

(ii)   Dear Mr ....

We have completed our investigation into the difficulties you were having with deliveries, and thank you for advising us of them.

The problem concerns our hauliers (transport company) who have had a number of strikes holding up deliveries to all their customers. However, the problem has been settled and they assure us (promise) that there will be no delays in future.

We regret the inconvenience this has caused you and can promise that your orders will be delivered on time. Please let us know if we can assist you in any other way.

Yours sincerely,

15.6 Unjustified complaints

Sometimes the customer's complaint is unjustified (wrong), and it is better to handle this by letter rather than on the phone to avoid arguments. And as complaints have to be investigated anyway, it will usually take time before the customer can get an answer.

(a)   Let the customer know what has happened:

We have now looked into (investigated) your complaint in your letter of (date) concerning (goods or service)

Thank you for your letter of (date) in which you told us about (complaint)

(b)   Tell the customer what has been done:

Our engineers, who visited you on the 9th October, have reported back to us and say that the photocopier you have been using has been left on overnight and this has burnt the motor out . . .

Our laboratory has examined the tee shirts you returned and tell us that shrinking was caused by washing in boiling water, which the instructions on each garment warn you not to do

(c)   Explain in tactful terms that you cannot accept the complaint:

Under these circumstances we cannot accept responsibility and therefore, will not be able to offer you a replacement or refund

Unfortunately we will not be able to offer compensation (money back) as the machine was damaged outside the terms of the guarantee

(d)   You should still thank the customer for writing to you:

Thank you for writing to us . . .

Thank you for contacting us about this matter

Exercise 73

Put the **prepositions** in this letter which is from a customer complaining to an accounts department about continuous overcharges on his monthly statements:

Dear Mr Davis,

I am writing ....¹ you to complain ...² overcharges made ...³ my monthly statements.
....⁴ the past three months I have received statements ...⁵ you asking ...⁶ ...⁷ $300.000 and $600.000 which was not due ...⁸ you. This has happened because credit notes and payments have been left ...⁹ instead of being put ....¹⁰ and always ...¹¹ your favour. I want your assurance that these errors will stop ....¹² now, or I will have to take my business ....¹³ another supplier.

Yours sincerely,

Exercise 74

Complaints often concern damage. Which **adjective** from the list below, is used for the damage the phrases are describing?

1 lost colour in sun 2 got smaller after washing 3 like a record left near heater 4 like metal plate hit with hammer 5 like plate of glass hit with hammer 6 material not folded properly 7 unwanted fold in material 8 like car windscreen after stone has gone through it 9 like broken stick 10 like paper pulled suddenly 11 unwanted mark on paper of material from liquid 12 like a cardboard box after heavy load falls on it 13 like iron left in water for months 14 like a cup with damaged rim 15 like damaged crockery with lines across them 16 two colours giving an unwanted colour 17 piece of string tied round itself in different places 18 opposite of tight 19 liquid completely going through material 20 dirt covering books or bookcases 21 worn out cuffs and collars on shirts and blouses

chipped	cracked	shrunk	faded	discoloured	loose
knotted	stained	shattered	frayed	dusty	drenched
(saturated)	crushed	torn	creased	smashed	wrinkled
dented	rusted (oxidised)		snapped	warped	

Exercise 75

Choose one of the three expressions which are in reply to a customers comment:

Example: 'The paper keeps crumpling in the copier'
          (a) that's unusual   (b) what d'you know about that   (c) well it's never happened before

Answer: (a)

1 'I washed the sweater and it shrank.'
   (a) Oh yes!   (b) could you tell me how you washed it?   (c) I bet you boiled it!
2 'I'd like to complain about a typewriter I bought from you.'
   (a) When?   (b) What's wrong with it?   (c) Could I have your name and address please?
3 '. . . well, that's the complaint.'
   (a) Nothing I can do about it   (b) I can't help you myself, but I'll pass the details on to someone who can   (c) Most of our machines are like that, they're not made here y'know.

4 'I'm phoning to complain about a faulty RX100.'
  (a) Can you give me details of the fault   (b) Why?   (c) Not my department.
5 'If the machine can't be repaired, what happens?'
  (a) We'll replace it   (b) Well, it may be replaced, or you might be offered a
  credit note, but the manager will make that decision   (c) Well, first we'll take a
  look at it, see if it's your fault that it doesn't work, if not, you get a refund.
6 'This is the fourth time I've received a wrong statement.'
    (a) Well, that's accounts for you   (b) Isn't that the way life is? (c) That must
  be very inconvenient, I'll check with accounts . . .
7 'You know, your company's getting a bad reputation!'
  (a) Could you give me more details of the fault   (b) Who says so?   (c) About
  what?
8 '. . . so as soon as the engineer explained it, I realised that it was my fault the
  machine hadn't been working properly.'
  (a) Well, those engineers know their job   (b) Thank you for calling us,
  anyway   (c) Well, don't make the same mistake next time.
9 '. . . what d'you mean you've got to get the file! I can't hang on to this phone
  forever!'
  (a) Then, can I call you back in a moment?   (b) You can call us later   (c) Why
  not? I've got to get the file.
10 'Your delivery service is terrible!'
  (a) We use a haulier, so it's not our fault   (b) I'll make enquiries with our hauliers
  immediately   (c) Our hauliers are the ones that are terrible.

Travel arrangements

Executives (company representatives) travel in their own countries or overseas to visit customers; inspect branches of their companies; take part in or visit exhibitions where they can see international companies' developments; attend company or international conferences where businessmen, scientists, politicians or technicians meet, listen to talks, and later make contact with one another to exchange ideas; or to visit their agents (their overseas representatives) who sell their company's products and services.

Executives' personal secretaries usually make arrangements for their **itinerary** (which is the programme for their trip) fixing travel arrangements, by road, rail, sea or air, and hotel accommodation, working out arrival and departure times.

They will also note addresses and phone and telex numbers where their executives can be reached or mail can be forwarded, and fix up (arrange) social and business appointments.

As well as this, they have to make sure the executive's **passport** is in order, and sometimes get a **visa** (special entry permission) to visit certain countries in, say, the Eastern Bloc (the communist countries). Visas are issued (given) by embassies or consulates in the executive's own country.

Medical arrangements might also have to be seen to, for **vaccinations** (injections for protection) against certain diseases, and **insurance** against illness, accident, loss of luggage, or damage to personal property would also have to be fixed up.

Currency or facilities to obtain money overseas will be arranged with the home banks. **Traveller's cheques**, which allow money to be exchanged abroad (overseas), **circular letters of credit**, which allow money to be taken from local banks abroad, and **international credit cards**, like 'Barclaycard' and 'Midland Bank's Mastercard International' will have to be obtained.

The executive's expenses may be **advanced** by his company (given before the trip), or he may make an **expense account statement** on his return, and draw money from **petty cash** or a special expense account for travelling purposes. The executive will be expected to hand in all **receipts** and **bills** from hotels and restaurants to account for (explain) what the money was paid for, so his or her company can claim this back in tax allowances from the government. A certain allowance is made for expenses where there would be no receipt or bill, e.g. taxi fares, and tips.

16.2 Methods of travelling

Before we go into 'methods of travelling', road, rail, air and sea, we should briefly look at international time-tables.

The 24 hour clock

Most time-tables in the world now are listed on a **24 hour clock**. This runs from 00.01 a.m. (**ante meridiem**, or morning) to 24.00 hours, p.m. (**post meridiem**, or midnight). So if a plane leaves at 05.30 hours, that will be at 5.30 a.m. (in the morning). If it arrives at 17.20, it arrives at 5.20, in the afternoon, destination time, of the country the executive will arrive in.

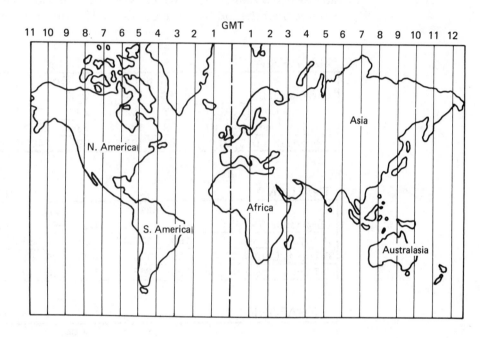

Algeria	GMT	Grenada	−4	New Zealand	+12
Argentina	−3	Guyana	−3	Nigeria	+1
Australia	+8 to +10	Hong Kong	+8	Norway	+1
Austria	+1	Hungary	+1	Portugal	+1
Bahrain	+3	Iceland	−1	Saudi Arabia	+3
Barbados	−4	India	+5½	Sierra Leone	GMT
Belgium	+1	Indonesia	+7 to +9	Singapore	+7½
Bermuda	−4	Iran	+3½	Spain	+1
Brazil	−3	Iraq	+3	Sweden	+1
Canada	−3½ to −8	Italy	+1	Switzerland	+1
China	+8	Jamaica	−5	Tanzania	+3
Cyprus	+2	Japan	+9	Trinidad &	
Denmark	+1	Kenya	+3	Tobago	−4
Egypt	+2	Kuwait	+3	Turkey	+2
France	+1	Libya	+2	Uganda	+3
Germany	+1	Malawi	+2	USA	−5 to −9
Ghana	GMT	Malaysia	+7½ to +8	USSR	+3
Greece	+2	Mexico	−6	Zambia	+2
Greenland	−3	Netherlands	+1	Zimbabwe	+2

Fig. 94 Time difference in countries round the world (+ ahead of GMT; − behind GMT)

To transfer to a 24 hour clock time, we simply take 12 from 24 to give us post meridiem (p.m.) time. 17.20 − 12.00 = 5.20 p.m. If a plane leaves at 16.40 and arrives at 19.35, we do the same sum, i.e. 16.40 − 12.00 = 4.40 p.m.; 19.35 − 12.00 = 7.35 p.m., so departure will be at 4.40 p.m. and arrival, 7.35 p.m.

To reverse the times (change them back) we just *add* 12.00. The plane leaves at 3.35 p.m. and arrives at 6.25 p.m. − add 12.00 departure 15.35, arrival 18.25.

Remember time changes as you move through **time zones**. Universal time is called **Greenwich Mean Time** (GMT) and is the time taken from the sun at Greenwich, London. However, in the UK, GMT is used in winter months and British Summer Time (which is one hour ahead of GMT) is used in the summer months and is the same as Central European Time.

MALAYSIA
1 Apr 85–31 Mar 86

Local tax at 0%	3 days US$	3 days £	7 days US$	7 days £	Extra days US$	Extra days £
B Toyota Corolla (AC, R)	118	102.61	246	213.91	35	30.43
D Galant Sigma (AC, R)	159	138.26	336	292.17	48	41.74
E Mazda 626 (AC, R)	184	160.00	399	346.96	57	49.57

THAILAND
1 Apr 85–31 Mar 86

Local tax at 0%	3 days US$	3 days £	7 days US$	7 days £	Extra days US$	Extra days £
A Toyota Corolla	150	130.43	296	257.39	43	37.39
C Toyota Corona 1800	200	173.91	400	347.83	58	50.43
E Toyota Crown Deluxe	259	225.22	519	457.30	74	64.35

SINGAPORE
1 Apr 85–31 Mar 86

Local tax at 0%	3 days US$	3 days £	7 days US$	7 days £	Extra days US$	Extra days £
B Nissan Sunny DX (AC, R)	138	120.00	277	240.87	41	35.65
D Datsun Bluebird (AC, R)	176	153.04	349	303.48	50	43.48
E Honda Accord (A) (AC, R)	241	209.57	482	419.13	68	59.13

USA–EAST
1 Jul 85–31 Aug 85

States: New York	3-7 days US$	3-7 days £	Extra days US$	Extra days £
A Chevrolet Chevette	174	151.30	44	38.26
C Chevrolet Citation	199	173.04	50	43.48
E Chevrolet Celebrity	236	205.22	59	51.30

Fig. 95 Car hire charges

Time changes must be considered when working out departure and arrival times.

Road travel

Very few executives travel by national or international coaches (buses) although they are half the price of rail fares, as the time used in travelling could be more useful to them in business, and most bus journeys will be at least twice as long as rail journeys.

However, executives might use their own cars, or company cars and claim **mileage expenses**. On very long distances the railways provide a 'Motorail' service which picks up cars and passengers between cities at a cost which would be almost the same as petrol and motorway or Autobahn charges (charges for using long fast roads). There are also **car ferries** (boats or hovercrafts) which will take vehicles across seaways, e.g. England to France, Greece to Turkey.

It is possible for a traveller from London to drive to Dover, get a ferry to a port in France, have his car put on a Motorail and taken down to Nice in the South of France.

Cars can also be hired by people who have had a driving licence for over a year, and are over 21 years old. The vehicle is picked up at the airport they will arrive in, and used, then returned to a place agreed between them and the car rental company. A list of typical car-hire charges is shown in fig. 95.

Rail travel

Most countries have fast inter-city (between city) rail travel facilities which offer regular service, special **off peak** (non rush hour) reduced prices, and for long distances or international travel reservations (advanced bookings) for seats, sleeping berths (beds), and restaurants and entertainment such as videos.

Season tickets, and circular tour tickets, which allow passengers to get off between journeys and board again without buying another ticket have improved the convenience (ease and comfort) of rail travel.

Fig. 96 is a special 'Nightrider Service' offered by British Rail for people going from London to Scotland. The map illustrates the route, the time-table gives arrival and departure times.

In many countries rail and air travel co-ordinate (work together) arrival and departure times so that passengers do not have to wait for a long time for connections, and mainline stations are close to, or part of the **air terminals** (passenger collection points where travellers are taken by bus to the airport). There are also non-stop services linking cities to airports.

Air travel

Airlines run domestic (home) and international flights on fixed schedules (set times and routes), and as more smaller independent companies open to compete with the big international airlines, the cost of travelling is being

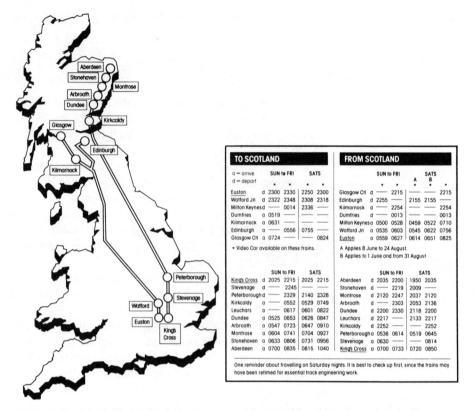

Fig. 96 British Rail's Nightrider Service at fares reduced to less than half price
(*Courtesy of British Railways Board*)

reduced, while the standard of regular service and passenger comforts are the same.

Reservations can be made through a travel agent, or direct with the airline, even by phone, but collection and payment for tickets has to be done within a certain time. Large companies have accounts with airlines or agencies, and by giving a code number can be charged for flights later.

Passengers **checking in** have their baggage weighed at a **checking-in desk**, and all airlines have limits on baggage weight for safety. The passenger's ticket is checked for 'take off' time and route, and there is a departure lounge to wait in until the flight is **called** over the 'public address system'.

Travellers can keep 'hand luggage' with them, but heavier cases are taken by 'handlers' to the plane and collected at the end of the journey from a 'carousel' (a roundabout) that delivers baggage.

Sea travel

As air travel has grown, sea travel has shrunk and is mainly for cruises (holidays). But reservations (bookings) are made a long time in advance of the trip, with two, three, or four berth (bed) cabins offered to travellers along with the full 'hotel service' of the shipping lines.

Exercise 76   The following questions are based on the illustrations in this Unit.

Fig 94

1   If it is 08.00 in London, what time is it in Jamaica?
2   What time would you have to adjust your watch to if it showed 15.00 GMT and
     you suddenly arrived in Malaysia?
3   If it is 8.30 a.m. in London, what time is it in Nigeria?
4   At 18.45 London time, the time in Singapore would be?

Fig 95

5   In pounds sterling, how much does it cost to rent a Chevrolet Chevette in New
     York for 7 days?
6   Is there a local tax for renting cars in Malaysia?
7   How much would it cost to rent a Datsun Bluebird in Singapore for 8 days, in
     US dollars?
8   What would be the rental, in pounds sterling for a Mazda 626 for 12 days in
     Malaysia? If the car company gave your firm a 10% discount on the rental,
     what would the net cost be to the nearest 1p.

Fig. 96

9   From the timetable, what times do the trains leave Kings Cross Sundays to
     Fridays?
10   What times do trains from Aberdeen arrive in Kings Cross on Saturdays?
11   What is the latest time trains leave Dundee from Saturday to Sunday?
12   If I catch the 22.15 from Glasgow, how long will it take me to arrive in Euston,
     London, if the express gets in at 06.27?

Exercise 77   Here is a conversation between James Raul and his secretary, Linda, discussing
arrangements she has made for him to visit Singapore. Choose the **correct word**
or **expression** from the three alternatives:

MR. RAUL: 'Can you give me[1] **news|instances|details** of the[2]
   journey|trips|arrangements you've made for me?'
LINDA: 'I've got them here. You have a[3] **part|reservation|reserve** on 08.30 from
   Heathrow, London, to Singapore.'
MR. RAUL: 'Heathrow's outside of London.'
LINDA: 'Yes, so you can[4] **get|have|make** a taxi to Victoria, the air[5]
   port|station|terminal and an airways[6] **bus|lorry|van** will collect you with the
   other passengers and take you to the airport. You'll have to be at Heathrow by
   07.30, one hour before[7] **take-off|take-over|take-on** so you can[8] **check
   in|check over|check through**, have your[9] **baggages|baggage|luggages**
   weighed, and ticket inspected. Then you'll have to wait in the[10]
   leaving|departure|waiting lounge until your flight is[11]
   named|defined|called.'
MR. RAUL: 'Is this the[12] **item|indent|itinerary** of my stay in Singapore?'
LINDA: 'Yes, everything's in that envelope. All your appointments, your[13] **travelling
   cheques|traveller's checks|traveller's cheques** and the managing director
   told me to remind you to[14] **bring back|take back|hold back** all receipts for
   your expense account.'
MR. RAUL: 'There's no[15] **vista|visa|visor** in my passport.'
LINDA: 'You don't need one for Singapore, and as you only had a[16]
   vacation|holiday|vaccination a few weeks ago you'll not need another for
   this trip. And this time don't forget to[17] **re-do|reset|remain** your watch and

put it seven and a half hours[18] **forward|backward|around** as you'll have to add on time once you're there.'

MR. RAUL: 'What about car hire?'

LINDA: 'I've arranged for a Datsun Bluebird to be waiting for you; all you have to do is inform the car hire firm and[19] **pick it up|put it down|leave it off** once you get[20] **into|onto|out of** the airport. The car's[21] **ready|available|working** for the three weeks you'll be there.'

MR. RAUL: 'Well you seemed to have[22] **seen|seen to|seen off** everything. And I see I'll be staying in the International Hotel. Good. I like it there.'

LINDA: 'You've a reservation from the 2nd to 23rd of May inclusive (including those dates)'

MR. RAUL: 'Is there anything you'd like me to bring you from there.'

LINDA: 'How about some warm weather, it's freezing here for this time of the year.'

16.3 Hotels and reservations

There are various types of accommodation for visitors to countries and cities.

Small hotels, **guest houses**, are usually no more than very large houses run by a family. **Motels**, usually situated near motorways, or freeways, are for travellers staying for a short time and offer a central dining place and lounges, with visitors staying in chalets. There are also **hostels**, which can be small places for hikers (people on walking holidays) or much larger places centred in cities with very modern conveniences and lounges and dining rooms.

The hotels where executives stay are what most people imagine hotels to be, large multi-storey buildings, in the middle of a city, and run by a full staff of administrators, caterers (people who deal with food), and chambermaids, who take care of visitors' rooms.

There are five generally accepted grades of hotels classified as one, two, three, four, or five star. The one star hotel offers the basic facilities of room, shared bathroom, and dining room, and this is often a guest house, then there is the five star Hilton and Savoy category, with all the conveniences a guest could want from swimming pools to casinos and highly trained staff offering personal service.

Services besides accommodation

Larger hotels are often used as **conference centres** for business or political gatherings (meetings) and offer a full range of conference facilities such as halls for meetings, public address systems, screens for slides and films, and catering (making and serving food) for buffets (where people take food from tables and walk around and meet one another) and set meals.

Exhibitions are held in these hotels, as well, and **staff dinner and dances** and **annual celebrations** can be arranged with the banqueting facilities being taken over for an evening.

Large rooms can be booked for meetings, presentations, demonstrations, and even interviews where there are a lot of candidates for a number of jobs and the company wants to show films and give lectures about itself and the jobs being offered.

Bookings

Bookings have to be well in advance of the date(s) that visitors want to stay, or organisers want to use the hotel facilities for, as, like most businesses, there are busy seasons for hotels, and though the ones in holiday resorts (places) have their 'high season' in spring, summer, and at public holiday times, the city hotels are booked throughout the year with individual reservations and **block bookings** (group bookings).

Letters, telexes and cables will often be enough to reserve a room, but a deposit (about 10 per cent of the total cost of accommodation) will have to be sent to 'confirm' the reservation.

If the company or guest is a regular customer, then a phone call might be sufficient to book accommodation, but the hotel will still expect a deposit to follow within a specified (stated) time.

Customers can book for **full pension** (full board : room, breakfast, lunch and evening meal) or **demi-pension** half board : room, breakfast, and evening meal).

Extra facilities, like private showers and baths, personal TV or video, a suite (a group of rooms) personal outside phone etc., are all added to the cost of accommodation, and have to be specifically (particularly) requested in the booking.

Here is a company letter booking accommodation for Mr. James Raul, the executive visiting Singapore in exercise 77.

UNIVERSAL COMPUTERS PLC

Tel: 2431 95333
London Office:
01 362 9815

ICP House
Milfords Road
Middlesex TW16 7HR

Telex: 781635
Telex: London
910831

The Manager
International Hotel
Jurong Port Road
Singapore 2261

8 April 19..

Dear Mr. Tang,

Reservation Confirmation

I would like to confirm our telex booking of this morning for a
single room with bath, shower, and private telephone, for one of
our executives, Mr. James Raul.
The reservation is for full board from 2 to 23 May 19.. inclusive.
I am also confirming the reservation for a small conference room
to be available on 14 May, when Mr. Raul will be holding a meeting
with fifteen of our South East Asian agents.
Please find enclosed our bank draft (No. 4718 65913 799845)
for US $1560.00 as a deposit. The balance will be paid as soon
as we receive your written confirmation of the booking.
We look forward to hearing from you soon.

Yours sincerely,

Linda Aaron

Linda Aaron

Personal secretary to James Raul

Encl. Midland bank draft

Fig. 97 A letter confirming a hotel reservation

Here are the telexes exchanged between Linda Aaron, James Raul's secretary and the International Hotel which arranged the booking.

(i) To the International Hotel

```
INOTEL

LONDON 910831



REQ. S/ROOM BTH SHWR PVTE PHNE FROM 2 TO 23 MAY THIS YR AND
.MLL CUNFNCE RM ON 14 MAY FR MR JAMES RAUL .
IF PUSS WILL SEND 10 O/O   DEPOSIT WITH LTTR C   BKG +?

  ONDON 910831
 INOTEL
```

Fig. 98 Telex making a booking

(ii) Reply from International Hotel

```
LONDON 910831
INOTEL

HAVE RESERVED ACCMDN FOR JAMES RAUL WITH FACILS REQ. PLSE SEND
$1560.00 US AS 10 O/O DEP BY BNK DRFT FOR BKG OF S/RM FROM
2 TO 23 MAY AND CNFRNCE RM ON 14 MAY SEND CFMG LTTR SOONEST ++

N TANG MNGR
LONDON 910831
INOTEL
```

Fig. 99 Telex confirming a booking

Exercise 78

Hotels use signs to indicate the facilities they offer. What do you think the following signs mean?

Exercise 79

Your answerback code is 889160 and you are telexing the Hong Kong Grand Hotel, telex 991453 HK to ask them to extend (lengthen) a booking for Mrs. Carol Dunn who has reserved a room from 9th July to 16th July inclusive, and would now like to stay until 23rd July. Explain that the additional deposit of $720.00 US will be sent with your letter confirming the booking.

Exercise 80

As the Hong Kong Grand Hotel, reply that Mrs. Dunn's room will be available for the extra time provided (as long as) the deposit is sent within two days by bank transfer.

Exercise 81

Your company, ARC Ltd., would like to book the main conference room in the Metropolitan Hotel for their annual representatives' meeting on 15th August this year.

There will be 50 people attending and the conference will be held from 09.00 to 17.00, with an hour for lunch from 12.30 to 13.30, and you would like the hotel to provide a four course 'sit down' menu for you, as well as refreshments (coffee and biscuits) for fifteen-minute breaks in the morning and afternoon.

You also want to know if they can provide a projector and screen, and sound equipment.

What would *you* say in the following conversation with the manager?

MANAGER: 'This is Mr. Wheelan, the manager, here, can I help you?'

YOU: '. . .' (introduce yourself and explain who you are phoning for)

MANAGER: 'What can I do for you?'

YOU: 'My company would . . . on . . . and . . . we will need a conference room . . .'

MANAGER: 'Will the conference take place all day?'

YOU: 'Yes, from . . . to . . . and we would like you . . . menu, and if possible . . . for two . . . Could you also arrange for . . . which is the equipment we will need during the conference?'

MANAGER: 'Yes, we'll be able to do that as many conferences are held here.'

YOU: 'Could you . . . ?' (ask for confirmation and a choice of three menus, plus the tariff (bill) to cover all expenses)

MANAGER: 'Yes, I'll do that. But would you please book as early as possible as this is our busy season, and when booking would you send a fifteen per cent deposit, with the cheque made out to 'Metropolitan Hotel Group', and crossed 'And Co?'

Exercise 82

Say whether these statements are *true* or *false*

		True	False
1	The plural for accommodation is accommodation**s**	☐	☐
2	The abbreviation **a.m.** is used before 12.00 hours	☐	☐
3	**Demi-pension** means part or half board	☐	☐
4	19.40 hours is 'twenty minutes to six' p.m.	☐	☐
5	B.S.T. means British Spring TIme	☐	☐
6	A 'ferry' can carry cars	☐	☐
7	A 'domestic air service' is for internal flights	☐	☐
8	A **guest house** is a large four star hotel	☐	☐
9	A hotel's 'high season' is its least busy period	☐	☐
10	There are no charges for extra facilities in hotels	☐	☐
11	Some countries do not require 'visas'	☐	☐
12	A vaccination is a holiday in the sun	☐	☐
13	A 'tariff' means a charge	☐	☐
14	Hotels 'cater' for parties	☐	☐
15	The best hotels are marked with a star	☐	☐

BASIC OFFICE ENGLISH

Exercise 83   Put the country, city, and currency together
Example: England; Manchester; Sterling

Countries

USSR	Italy	Greece	Yugoslavia	Japan
USA	Germany	Norway	Australia	Brazil
India	Thailand	Malaysia	Israel	Canada
Jordan	France	Saudi Arabia	Venezuela	Turkey

Cities

Bangkok	Calcutta	Kuala Lumpur	Rio de Janeiro	Jeddah
Hamburg	Melbourne	Paris	Amman	Caracas
Bergen	Kobe	Vancouver	Milan	Washington
Moscow	Salonika	Tel Aviv	Dubrovnik	Istanbul

Currencies

Dollar	Dinar	Rupee	Rial	Baht
Franc	Bolivar	Dollar	Dinar	Yen
Ringgit	Krona	Rouble	Deutschmark	Dollar
Lira	Lira	Shekel	Cruzeiro	Drachma

UNIT 17

Office safety

In most countries there are laws to protect workers in commerce and industry against injuries or death. In the UK the Health and Safety at Work Act of 1974 (HASAWA) protected office workers in particular and made both employers and employees (workers) responsible for safety and security.

In many companies there is a 'safety committee' which reports to the management at various times on safety problems which affect their colleagues (fellow workers). For example a machine may have been brought in which people think is dangerous to use, or dangerous to have in an office where a lot of people are working; or a material such as asbestos (used for fire proofing, but which can cause cancer) has been discovered.

Safety committees not only protect employees, but employers themselves, as injury or illness can be expensive if the person who is harmed (hurt) sues the company (takes them to court) and makes them pay compensation (money to make up for the injury) for what has happened to them.

17.1 Accident prevention

Most accidents in offices are caused by negligence (not taking care of something) or carelessness (not taking care when doing something). Knowing that a situation could be dangerous, and doing something about it could prevent over ninety per cent of the accidents at home and in work.

Fire: Firemen say that fires do not 'happen', they are caused, and could be prevented.

Fire

Cigarettes could not only be dangerous to *your* health but to other peoples' if you are not careful.

No Smoking

Never smoke in a non-smoking area, or when using inflammables (easily lit materials) such as cleaning fluids and spirits. Always put cigarettes out and matches in an ashtray and make sure they are out.

Empty waste-paper baskets regularly – a match or cigarette end not put out (extinguished) properly will cause a fire.

No naked lights

Never leave papers or spirits near open heaters (electric bar heaters), or leave them behind a heater.

Learn to use fire extinguishers – the instructions are usually on the side. And find out where your fire exits (escapes) are. Make sure fire doors are always closed, and there is nothing in front of them to prevent people escaping.

If you *smell* burning, gas, burning rubber, or a smell like bad fish report it to your supervisor or manager immediately. If you *see* flames, try to put

Alarm sign

Electricity

General
warning
of danger

Wires

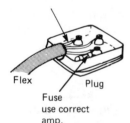

Flex

Plug

Fuse
use correct
amp.

Adaptor
and 2 plugs

Power
point (socket)

them out with an extinguisher only. If they get out of control go to an alarm and set it off (they are usually fixed on walls and covered by glass). Break the glass and press the bell or buzzer.

Oxygen, wind and air, feeds fires, so close, do *not* lock, doors and windows. And if you are caught in a fire, never throw a door open to escape – this could cause a 'flash fire' with the wind exploding the flames at you.

All companies have fire instructions on notice boards and walls. Read them, they could save your own and other peoples' lives.

Electricity: If a machine does not work, call maintenance. Do not try to fix it yourself. If a machine is overheating (getting too hot), turn it off. If there is a strange smell coming from it, turn it off. If the smell is like bad fish, then the plug connecting it to the power is burning. Turn the machine off and pull the plug out.

If a fuse in the plug had burned out, make sure the one you replace it with is suitable for that appliance. If it is too strong, you may not realise there is a fault and this could cause a fire. Never touch an uncovered wire (with the metal showing) if the plug is connected. Never use anything other than the right tool to fix electrical appliances. If in doubt, call maintenance.

Adaptors are appliances that allow more than one plug to work off the same point so that two or three machines can be run at the same time from the same point. Never overload (put too many plugs) in one adaptor. Maintenance will tell you the maximum number you can use. Never run an appliance from the wrong source of power, e.g. plugging an electric kettle into a light **socket** (the place where the light bulb is fitted).

Never leave water, a bucket or glass, near any power source (wall socket), wire, or plug, even if the plug is not connected.

Don't ever play with electric fans. If they start suddenly they will cut your fingers off, or shatter and the flying splinters can cause serious injuries.

The main rule for electricity is, *if you are not absolutely certain of what you are doing, call an electrician.*

Filing cabinets: Always make sure drawers are closed. Fill cabinets up from the bottom drawer. If the top and second drawers are filled first the cabinet will topple over (fall over) when drawers are pulled out.

Drawers left open can trip people (catch their feet and make them fall), or jam into them (stab them) if they are carrying something and do not see the drawer.

Trips, spills and falls: Make sure **carpets** and **linoleum** are all in good repair and flat to prevent people tripping. Chairs are for 'sitting on', not standing on to reach the top of a shelf. Standing on a swivel (turning) chair can cause a serious accident. Do not lean back on chairs, resting them on two instead of four legs. Head and back injuries are often caused by this.

If something is broken, a desk, chair, machine etc., remove it, or put a note on it saying 'Do not use'.

Never block corridors outside the offices with anything, even for a minute. Keep gangways between desks clear so people will not trip over things.

Do not hang coats over the backs of chairs, or let a flex trail across a room, when carrying something like an electric typewriter.

Make sure things are not left hanging over desks or sticking out (protruding), and that liquids on desks cannot be knocked over to spill onto work that may have taken days to prepare – two days work can be ruined by a spilt cup of coffee.

A few days work
can be ruined by
spilt coffee

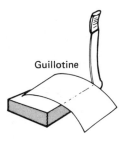

Guillotine

If you have long hair, very loose sleeves, or wear a pendant, be careful when using automatic machines which can catch loose things.

Never throw open doors, particularly swing doors, as you can smash into somebody and seriously hurt them.

Do not leave books on window ledges, particularly by open windows. If there are plants (flowers) make sure they are secure.

Cutting and slicing: Guillotines (for cutting paper) should always have guards on them as they can cause serious permanent injuries to fingers if they are not used properly or guarded correctly.

Scissors, staplers, especially electric staplers must be handled with care.

Put drawing pins, paper clips etc., in boxes, and if they fall on the floor, pick them up. If you break any glass, wrap it first, then put it in a waste-paper bin, and make sure *all* the pieces have been found.

17.2 Health and hygiene

Offices should be well lit, with good overhead lighting, ventilated with good heating equipment for cold weather. They should be clean with sufficient toilet and washing facilities for all the staff.

Different countries have different laws to make sure employers give their staff reasonable working conditions, and health and safety committees, which we mentioned earlier, can be organised to inform employers when problems arise.

Toilet systems that do not work properly, bad water, lack of soap, paper, or towels can all be health hazards (dangers). Worn carpets, broken appliances, damaged furniture, etc., can all cause injuries, which can be avoided if they are repaired in time.

If a person does become ill, or injured, you should know where the *First Aid* box is kept, so you can get bandages, plasters, antiseptic (anti-infection) creams or liquids, or pain relieving pills. A basic knowledge of First Aid, teaching you how to treat cuts, bruises, fainting, and breaks, is always useful to know anywhere you go. A book, or even evening classes would help you learn First Aid.

Fig. 100 An illustration of the possible dangers in an office

Exercise 84

This is a memorandum to staff on what they should do if there is a fire in the building. Read the memo, then answer the questions on it.

MEMORANDUM

To: All Staff
From: Security
Date: 16 April 19..

FIRE INSTRUCTIONS

1   If you discover a fire inform the switchboard or reception on internal extensions 615 or 616. Give them the location and state of the fire. They will call the fire department

2   Only use extinguishers to put out the blaze, otherwise close the door on the fire and inform everyone nearby

3   Sound the alarm which is a continuous siren

4   Do not panic

5   Do not collect anything from the offices

6   Do not use the lifts, only use fire escapes or stairways

7   Do not go back inside the building

BECOME FAMILIAR WITH EXTINGUISHERS AND FIRE ESCAPES THIS CAN SAVE YOUR LIFE AND THE LIVES OF OTHERS

---

1 Who should you contact if there is a fire?
2 Who will call the fire department?
3 What sound does the alarm make?
4 What should you do about personal possessions?
5 What general advice does the memo give to staff?

Exercise 85   Answer these questions using the **correct conditional**.

Example: If you saw someone smoking in a non-smoking area, what would you
              do?
Answer: If I saw someone smoking in a non-smoking area, I'd ask them to put
              their cigarette out.

1 If you saw a waste bin burning, what would you do?
2 What would you have done, if you had smelled gas?
3 If you didn't know how a fire extinguisher works, how would you find out?
4 If you are going to use a copier, and it overheats, what will you do?
5 What would happen if you put a fuse that was too strong into a plug?
6 What happens to filing cabinets if they are full at the top and empty in the bottom
  drawers?
7 What should you do if a machine is out of order or a piece of furniture is
  broken?
8 If you had broken that drinking glass, what would you have done?
9 What should a guillotine have, if you want to use it? (begin with Unless . . .)
10 What would you do if maintenance could not repair an appliance straight
   away?

17.3 Security   The degree of the company's security (how much security) that is needed
will depend on the type of work the company does. Travel agents and small
retailers (shopkeepers) will be more worried about money or goods being
stolen than protecting secrets. Government departments and large
industries are usually more worried about information and plans being
taken from them. In this case, there will be a general guide to employees
on how to protect security, and staff might be asked to sign a contract saying
they will not give any information about the company to those outside it.

In a security-sensitive organisation staff will protect all information no
matter how unimportant it may seem to them personally.

All records will be locked away when not being used, and this includes
tapes as well as written material. Carbons will also be looked after carefully,
as holding a carbon to a mirror can tell you what was typed.

Only general information about the company is given over the phone,
and only then if the person answering recognises the caller.

Giving any information to outsiders is forbidden.

Documents are not simply thrown away when they are no longer needed,
but shredded through a machine, see fig. 101.

Often staff will require passes to get into, and sometimes, out of the
building. And security will not allow any 'unauthorised person', someone
without permission, to come into the building.

Most companies pay any large amounts of money they might have into
a bank as soon as possible. And many smaller organisations that will have
a large amount of money by the evening, e.g. a store, will either use a
sophisticated safe, or an outside bank safe, for security.

Fig. 101 A shredder

Personal valuables

Personal belongings (your own property) should always be with you. You should not leave anything you value lying around, even for a moment. In many places it is easy for an outsider to walk in, take a purse or wallet, then walk out.

If a wrist-watch, ring, or pendant is taken off in a wash-room while washing, put it back on immediately.

Like the problem of safety, negligence and carelessness are usually responsible for office thefts – if the valuables are not there, then there is nothing to steal.

Finally, at the end of the day, all electrical appliances should be unplugged, or turned off, windows, desks, cabinets and doors locked.

Exercise 86

Choose the correct **singular** or **plural** forms in the sentences
1 The time-table information he gave us (are/is) useful.
2 The police (are/is) looking into the case of fraud.
3 Statistics (have/has) a way of confusing people.
4 The changes in the political system (are/is) going to affect overseas trade.
5 Four hundred dollars (is/are) not much money to earn for a month.
6 The recent news from our agents in Singapore (haven't/hasn't) been very hopeful.
7 They produce jeans which (are/is) very fashionable.
8 Do you think their advice on filing (has/have) been useful.
9 These binoculars (have/has) a special lens which (are/is) made in Hong Kong.
10 Neither of these suggestions (are/is) worth considering.

Abbreviations

Abbreviations are used in commerce and industry for fast communication. When you use an abbreviation you should make sure it is internationally recognised.

The trend (fashion) at present is to omit (leave out) stops in abbreviations, for example U.N. (United Nations) is now written UN, and when a country or organisation is not included, the lower case (small letters) are written – cif (cost, insurance, freight), rather than the upper case (capital letters) CIF.

Many English abbreviations are based on Latin, for example *anno domini* (AD). So when you see (l) in the explanations, it means the abbreviation has come from a Latin source.

Abbreviation	Explanation
&	and (ampersand)
a/c	account
AD	(1) *anno domini*(l), used in dating, e.g. AD1951, see also BC
advt(s)	advertisement(s)
a.m.	*ante meridiem*(l) – before 12.00 hours
asst	assistant
@	at, e.g. 3 @ $5
BC	before Christ, used in dating, e.g. 300 BC, see also AD
be	bill of exchange
b/f	brought forward, used in accounts
Bros.	brothers, e.g. Moss Bros. Ltd.
C	Centigrade
c	*circa*(l), meaning 'about that time', e.g. *circa* 1781.
caps	capital letters
cc	cubic centimetre or copies (to)
cif	cost, insurance, freight (a shipping charge)
c/f	carried forward, used in accounts, also 'carriage paid'
cm(s)	centimetre(s)
Co.	company, e.g. L. Smith & Co.
c/o	care of, used for letters, e.g. c/o J. Green. Also means carried over (to next page)
COD	cash on delivery
c/p	carriage paid
Cr	credit
cwo	cash with order
cwt(s)	hundredweight (there are 20 cwts in a non-metric ton)

dept	department
do.	ditto; the same (also ")
Dr	debit (also Doctor)
E & O E	Errors and omissions excepted
EEC	European Economic Community
EFTA	European Free Trade Association
encl(s).	enclosed; enclosures
e.g.	*exempli gratia*(l), for example, or example given
etc.	*et cetera*(l), and the others; and so on.
Esq.	Esquire, e.g. D. Brown Esq. but *not* Mr. D. Brown Esq.
F	Fahrenheit
fas	free alongside ship (shipping cost)
fig	figure, e.g. fig. 1, fig. 2 etc.
fob	free on board (shipping cost)
ft	foot or feet (non-metric measurement of distance)
g	gram (metric weight)
gal	gallon (non-metric liquid measurement)
GATT	General Agreement on Tariffs and Trade
GB	Great Britain (England, N. Ireland, Scotland, Wales)
GMT	Greenwich Mean Time (also BST British Summer Time, and UST, Universal Standard Time)
GPO	General Post Office (also PO, Post Office)
HP	hire purchase
h.p.	horse power
ib.	(or ibid) *ibidem*(l), in the same place
id.	*idem*(l), the same
i.e.	*id est*(l), that is
IMF	International Monetary Fund
Inc.	incorporated
K	computer abbreviation for 1000 bytes
kg(s)	kilogramme(s) (metric weight)
kl(s)	kilometre(s) (metric measurements of distance)
lat	latitude, horizontal map division
long	longitude, vertical map division
Ltd.	limited company, e.g. J.R. Black Ltd.
m(s)	metres (metric measurement of length)
memo(s)	memorandum(s) also memoranda plural
mm(s)	millimetre(s) (metric measurement of length)
misc.	miscellaneous
Mme	Madame
Messrs	Messieurs
mpg	miles per gallon (non-metric measurement for petrol use)
mph	miles per hour (non-metric measurement for speed, compare with kilometres per hour)
MS or MSS	manuscript
MV	motor vessel
NB	*nota bene*(l), note well, make a note of
No.(s)	*numero*(l), number(s)
OAS	Organisation of American States

OECD	Organisation for Economic Cooporation and Development
oz	ounce (non-metric weight)
p.a.	*per annum*(l), per year
PAYE	Pay As You Earn (UK tax system for employees)
p.c.	per cent
pd.	paid
p.m.	*post meridiem*(l), after 12.00 hours
pp	*per procurationem* (per pro) (l), on behalf of; for
pp	printed pages
PRO	Public Relations Officer
pro tem	*pro tempore*(l), for the time being
pt(s)	pint (non-metric liquid measurement)
PTO	please turn over
PS	*postscriptum*(l), an addition to a letter, also for a further addition PPS
QED	*quot erat demonstrandum*(l), which was to be proved – usually used after a mathematical theory
R/D	refer to drawer
recd.	received
rpm	revolutions per minute – for machinery
RSVP	*répondez s'il vous plait*(f) – reply please
S or R	Sale or return
sec	secretary
SI	*Système International d'Unités*(f), International System of Units, the metric system
sic	so written – that is how it is written
soc	society
supt	superintendent
SS	steam/sail ship, e.g. the *SS Canberra*
STD	subscriber trunk dialling
stet	let it stand, do not change it
UK	United Kingdom (England, N Ireland, Scotland, Wales)
VAT	Value Added Tax
viz.	*videlicet*(l), namely, e.g. 'please send us a cheque for the outstanding balance viz. $2000.00
wk	week
yd	yard (non-metric measurement of length)
Yrs	Yours, e.g. yours faithfully.

Key to exercises

Exercise 1

1 (a) **2** no **3** 'a bright, lively person **4** 'there are prospects for advancement'. **5** (c) **6** Long hours; lot of work; no mention of pay or holidays; small company and may not stay in business long. **7** 3 weeks holiday per annum; staff bonus; Luncheon Vouchers; half-day release for studies **8** No, they asked you to phone. **9** 'must like working with figures'. **10** (a) general clerical assistant; (b) male or female; (c) a . . . person.

Exercise 2

1 position; vacancy; post; situation. **2** salary. **3** subsidised. **4** correspondence. **5** annual; per annum. **6** leave; vacation **7** negotiable = 'can be discussed'; increments = 'increases' **8** routine **9** prospects **10** advertising.

Exercise 3

Large **company** requires **clerk/typist** as **assistant** to **accounts manager** and to help with **general duties**. Salary $6000.00 **per annum**. 3 **weeks vacation per annum**. 5 days **per week. Hours** 9.00–5.00. **Luncheon Vouchers. Telephone 01 345 1171.**

Exercise 4

1 Should not put name over his address. **2** There is no date. **3** Indented address changed to block style. **4** No punctuation after 'Co.' and 'Ltd.' **5** Should thank company for sending Application Form. **6** Should refer to advertisement. **7** Should not use the contraction **'I've'**, but **I have**. **8** Carrer should be 'career'. **9 to hear** should be **to hearing**. **10** Should be **Yours faithfully** not **Yours sincerely**.

Exercise 5

Fill out application form.

Exercise 6

Correct spellings are: **1** application **2** necessary **3** receive **4** clerk **5** sincerely **6** faithfully **7** business **8** permanent **9** address **10** accounts **11** abbreviation **12** personnel **13** assistant **14** secondary.

Exercise 7

'I'd like to speak to Miss Mary Alabi please, it's about the advert for "a general assistant" with your agency.'
'I . . . my name is David Low, and I'd like to apply for the position you advertised in "The Daily News" for a "general assistant".'
'I am 17, and I live in Lagos . . . just finished my studies at the local technical college took an RSA in office practice.'
'I haven't got the results yet, but . . .'
'Yes, but I'm very interested in advertising and I don't mind working long hours.'
'I can come at any time.'
'Tomorrow afternoon at 2.30, that would be all right.'
'Yes, I'll be there at 2.30.'

Exercise 8

'Can I speak to Miss Terry White, please?'
'She is in personnel.'

'One, one, five, six.'

'Kim Lam, and you wrote to me on the 12th of July saying that I had been invited to/was to attend an interview with Mr. Leonard Green, the Personnel Manager, on Thursday the 25th of July at 10.00 a.m., and I'm phoning to confirm I can attend on that date.'

'Yes, it was LMG/TW.'

'Yes. I get out at Holborn station, then walk up Kingsway, across Theobald's Road, then turn left into Great Russell Street, and go into the store through the staff entrance in Bedford Way.'

'On the 9th floor.'

Exercise 9
1 . . . , if you dressed badly. **2** . . . they will employ you. **3** . . . , they will not interview you. **4** . . . , if I changed the interview date. **5** . . . , they will not understand you. **6** If you left early, . . . **7** . . . , I would tell you. **8** . . . , they will offer you a job. **9** If anyone likes working with figures, . . . **10** . . . , you should not apply for the job.

Exercise 10
1 (a) **2** (b) **3** (b) **4** (c) **5** (a) **6** (c) **7** (c) **8** (b) **9** (b) **10** (b)

Exercise 11
for; of; with; in; of; to; of; of; to; on; in; at.

Exercise 12
1 General Clerical Assistant **2** £4,524.00 **3** 9.00 a.m. to 5.00 a.m. **4** 3 weeks holiday plus public holidays **5** 10 days. Doctors certificate after 3 days absence. **6** Company has Non-Contributory Pension Scheme. **7** Disciplinary Action covered by Rules 1–20 in 'Staff Employment and Conditions of Work'.
8 One month's notice required either side.

Exercise 13
1 work **2** is **3** am always moving **4** am helping **5** am always moving **6** is
7 are constantly asking **8** sound **9** like **10** don't mind **11** am just grumbling
12 do **13** do **14** cannot do **15** are moving **16** start **17** get **18** work
19 arrive **20** Do they pay **21** come **22** give **23** are you planning to see
24 is **25** am seeing **26** am definitely asking **27** are getting **28** earn **29** am working

Exercise 14
1 e **2** j **3** g **4** m **5** a **6** i **7** n **8** b **9** c **10** o **11** d **12** f **13** h **14** p
15 l **16** k.

Exercise 15
1 selling **2** marketing **3** advertising **4** getting **5** manufacturing **6** packing
7 sending **8** handling **9** transporting **10** controlling **11** dealing **12** staying
13 writing **14** adding **15** subtracting **16** dividing **17** multiplying
18 working **19** working out **20** doing.

Exercise 16
1 'Can I help you?' **2** She put Miss Tam's name in a register. **3** 'Do you have an appointment?' **4** File it. **5** I **think** Mr Lee . . . **6** 'Reception here.' **7** They were not **available**. **8** 'It would be better . . .' **9** She repeated it. **10** '. . . tell me **exactly** what he . . .'

Exercise 17
unemployment; unusual; insecure; inexpensive; dissimilar; independent; uncontrolled; unreal; disorganised; unpack; disprove; indirect; unlike; dislike; inactive; unexpected; uninvited; disconnected; unsuccessful; unimpressed; disassociate; unhelpful.

Exercise 18
1 more **3** They did not fit the new models **3** 771 **4** Yes **5** Sales **6** No **7** 5th March.

Exercise 20

1 happened **2** did I see **3** heard **4** was **5** was **6** took **7** did not get **8** were always taking **9** were **10** were **11** was taking **12** were typing **13** were using **14** were walking **15** could not hear **16** was saying **17** was writing **18** interrupted **19** was delivering **20** did not get **21** was coming **22** was staying **23** did not sign **24** did not say **25** was **26** told **27** told **28** said **29** would tell **30** would you tell **31** told **32** knew **33** was **34** left **35** told **36** was.

Exercise 21

Alliance Bank Ltd
Arding & Hobbs Ltd
Au Yeung, Wang Hing
Bankers (The Institute of)
British Airways
C & A Ltd
Cawley, David
Change, Lawrence
Evergreen Publications Ltd.
H.M.S.O.
Kahn, Mohsin

MacAndrews, Ian
McKinnley, J
Malaysian Exports
Manning, Bernard
Marks & Spencer PLC
Masters, Helen
O'Malley, George
P & O Lines Ltd
Peters, Liv
Reed, Stephen
Rolls-Royce Ltd

Ruiz y Chanco, M
St. John, Brian
Sarawak Shipping Co.
Sato, Keiko
Smith, Abel
Smith, James
Tadokoro, A
Tesco
Tsai, Yuan
Zeidermann, J

Exercise 22

1 d; j; l **2** f **3** g; m; n **4** b; i **5** e **6** c **7** a **8** h.

Exercise 23

1 s; o; y; d **2** k; e; z **3** g; w; h **4** b; q **5** i; p; f **6** j; r; n **7** v; l; c **8** Miscellaneous — Gothenburg (Sweden); Kowloon (Hong Kong); Lisbon (Portugal); Peking (China); Tokyo (Japan).

Exercise 24

1 (c) **2** (b) **3** (c) **4** (a) **5** (b) **6** (c) **7** (a) **8** (c)

Exercise 25

1 Have you finished **2** have been using **3** have been dealing **4** have been putting **5** have just reached **6** haven't finished **7** asked **8** have been working **9** have been arranging **10** Have you ever worked **11** used **12** was **13** have never filed **14** have heard **15** had had **16** would have been **17** would have found **18** have finished **19** have you checked **20** have checked **21** have forgotten **22** have forgotten **23** forgot.

Exercise 26

1 Filing **2** to the 'Js' **3** Microfiche **4** micro-processor **5** no **6** That all the papers were in the file **7** She forgot to sign the Charge Out book **8** Her manager.

Exercise 27

1 Yes, every 6 months **2** Fiche and Rolls of film **3** $2,200.00 **4** No **5** Viewed on a screen.

Exercise 28

1 (a) **2.** (b) **3** (a) **4** (a) **5** (a) **6** (c).

Exercise 29

1 speak to someone **2** Jackson **3** Stores Manager **4** we could order **5** 'Litewate Shelves' Catalogue No. LS357 **6** any shelves of the same catalogue number, sizes 300 x 45 x 5 cm **7** deliver them within the next 10 days? **8** call round for them in that time **9** pay by cheque **10** we have an account with you **11** send an order **12** get/receive confirmation from you by letter, that you can supply the order **13** 10% discount **14** would be £144.00 **15** call me or Mr. Jackson.

Exercise 30

1A 10th February 19 . . **1B** Denby Manufacturing, 500 Li Chit Street, Wanchai, Hong Kong **1C** Mr. David Walton **2** Sales Manager **3** latest catalogue of summer dresses   **4** shops/stores   **5** summer   **6** price-list   **7** c.i.f.   **8** what trade discounts   **9** your delivery dates   **10** preparing for the summer season   **11** early   **12** urgent   **13** faithfully   **14** signature

Exercise 31

1 6 @ $300.00 = $1800.00; 5 @ $130.00 = $650; 1 @ $500.00 = $500.00   **2** Gross Total $2430.00   **3** Less 5% Cash Disc. ($121.50) = Net $2308.50.

Exercise 32

1 As soon as she **had typed** . . . she put it . . .   **2** When he **had got** . . . he put . . .   **3** After he **had been working** . . . , they dismissed him.   **4** I **had been living** . . . before I moved . . .   **5** She **had been working** . . . before they transferred her . . .   **6** I **had been studying** . . . before I understood . . .   **7** Although posted . . . I **had forgotten** . . .   **8** As soon as he **had left** . . . the phone rang.   **9** He **had been working** . . . when he realised . . .   **10** They **had been thinking** . . . before they finally went . . .

Exercise 33

1 (b)   **2** (b)   **3** (a)   **4** (c)   **5** (c)   **6** (b)   **7** (b)   **8** (c)   **9** (b)   **10** (c)

Exercise 34

1 Should be **Ltd** or **PLC**, not both   **2** 31st March should be 31st January   **3** Invoice 7156 should be in Debit column, not Credit   **4** Debit note DN541 should be **added** not subtracted   **5** Allowing for D/N error total should be £590.00 not £490.00   **6** O & EO should be E & OE   **7** Trade Discount should be **Cash Discount**.

Exercise 35

Yamada's address in centre or on the right. Okoronkwo's address above Dear . . .   **1** Okoronkwo   **2** enclosed   **3** Debit Note   **4** undercharge   **5** Invoice   **6** 5516A   **7** error/mistake   **8** extension   **9** @   **10** $1500.00   **11** $1300.00   **12** $200.00   **13** mistake/error   **14** debit   **15** statement   **16** inconvenienced   **17** sincerely   **18** Sales Manager.

Exercise 36

1 help   **2** enquiring   **3** invoice   **4** account   **5** ledger   **6** allowed   **7** trade   **8** credit   **9** makes   **10** $267.00   **11** $2403.00   **12** including   **13** net   **14** copy.

Exercise 37

1 False   **2** False   **3** True   **4** True   **5** False   **6** False   **7** True   **8** True   **9** False   **10** True   **11** False   **12** False   **13** False   **14** True   **15** False   **16** True   **17** True   **18** True   **19** True   **20** True.

Exercise 38

1 Bank branch number is wrong, should be 63-0982 not 63-0782   **2** No date on cheque   **3** Should be A.**C**. Holdings not A.**M**. Holdings   **4** In the writing of the amount 36p should be 63p   **5** In the crossing the words 'Barclays Bank, Holloway Road,' should appear as it is to be paid into the particular branch account.

Exercise 39

1 will you be sending   **2** will be posting   **3** will you have credited   **4** will have passed   **5** will be writing   **6** will have received   **7** will have left   **8** will be travelling   **9** will be writing   **10** will be going to   **11** will be staying   **12** will be travelling   **13** will be spending   **14** will you be coming   **15** will be coming   **16** will have finished   **17** will have made arrangements.

Exercise 40

Across. **2** Statement   **7** Has   **9** To   **10** Plan   **13** Aside   **15** Cash Point   **17** In   **18** Curriculum Vitae   **21** Rice   **22** Start   **23** Tray   **25** As   **28** Stationery   **31** Draw   **33** It   **34** Advice Note   **35** Dear
Down. **1** All   **2** Sincerely   **3** At   **4** To   **5** My   **6** That   **8** Seen   **10** Percentage   **11** Application   **12** Film   **14** Director   **16** Secure   **19** Train   **20** Air   **24** Added   **26** Sat   **27** Taxi   **29** One   **30** E & OE   **31** Your

Exercise 41

1 With/In **2** of **3** to **4** in **5** of **6** in **7** to **8** on **9** of **10** in **11** At **12** of **13** up **14** to **15** to **16** with **17** From **18** up **19** in/on **20** to **21** up **22** in **23** for

Exercise 42

1 (8) **2** (6) **3** (7) **4** $5.00 **5** $1.50 (9) **6** (5) **7** $11.60 (6) $2.40 (9) **8** (1) **9** Fo **10** $9.20 (5) 80¢ (9) **11** (8) **12** $2.25 (5), 45¢ (9) **13** (7) **14** (5) **15** (3)

Exercise 43

1 – **2** the **3** the **4** an **5** a **6** an **7** – **8** a **9** the **10** – **11** a **12** – **13** – **14** the **15** the **16** the **17** – **18** the **19** – **20** – **21** – **22** the **23** the **24** – **25** – **26** The **27** the **28** the **29** the **30** the **31** – **32** the **33** the **34** a **35** the **36** the **37** a **38** the **39** – **40** – **41** – **42** –

Exercise 44

1 l **2** i **3** b **4** q **5** h **6** k **7** g **8** a **9** m **10** d **11** j **12** o **13** e **14** c **15** f **16** n **17** p.

Exercise 45

1 (b) **2** (c) **3** (b) **4** (c) **5** (c) **6** (a) **7** (a) **8** (b) **9** (c) **10** (a).

Exercise 46

1 A mistake was made when the invoice was written out. We were overcharged and must be sent a credit note.
2 We are allowed a 10% discount by our customers when goods are bought in bulk
3 The canteen must not be used while it is being decorated
4 Cheque cards must be shown when goods are being paid for by cheque
5 It is said that . . . It is thought . . . But it is also believed . . .
6 These parcels must be taken to the post office, sent by registered post, signed for, and the receipt brought back
7 My pen was taken . . . my question wasn't answered, but it's being used.
8 A full banking service is offered by Girobank. Chequebook facilities can be used, payments transferred through the Girobank system, and money saved and interest given on Girobank savings accounts
9 The button marked 'On' is pressed, the machine is allowed to warm up, paper is put in the 'feed tray' and the document being photocopied is placed over the glass panel. The dial is set to the number of copies wanted, then the button marked 'Start' is pressed, then . . .
10 . . . the service department was called . . . the machine was taken apart and every piece examined. A new drum was put in then it was filled with 'toner'. They said the wrong sized paper was being used.

Exercise 47

1 False **2** True **3** False, it is A4 **4** True **5** True **6** True **7** False **8** False **9** False **10** True **11** True the word is stationary **12** True **13** False, a paper clip would be used **14** True **15** False **16** True **17** True **18** True **19** False **20** False, compare with No. 11

Exercise 48

1 Large companies buy stationery in bulk as they use it in large quantities and their suppliers give them discounts.
2 The manager told me . . . I gave it to him . . . he told me . . .
3 A manual typewriter can only type . . . , however, a word processor can 'run off' . . .
4 You sent us . . . we ordered . . . you delivered . . . can your delivery van collect . . . as we will not use them . . . ?
5 (a) . . . they did make you wait . . . ?
(b) They made me wait . . . before they saw me.
(c) When they interviewed you . . . did they ask you . . . ?

(d) . . . they asked me . . . how long the company employed me.

(e) How long did they interview you for?

(f) They did not interview me . . . they had to see . . . so they only interviewed me . . .

(g) . . . they will give you the job?'

(h) They will give me . . . , they saw . . .

(i) . . . what most impressed them?

Exercise 49 (a) diamond   (b) square   (c) circle   (d) triangle   (e) oblong   (f) drum/cylindrical   (g) pyramid   (h) cone/conical   (i) cube   (j) sphere/spherical

Exercise 50 Check against example on fig. 60. Stock balance should be June 8th, 18 reams; 16th 16 reams; 24th 13 reams so 37 reams had to be ordered on 25th June.

Exercise 51 **1** a   **2** –   **3** the   **4** the   **5** the   **6** the   **7** A   **8** a   **9** the   **10** a   **11** –   **12** The **13** the   **14** the   **15** the   **16** a   **17** the   **18** –   **19** the   **20** a   **21** the   **22** a **23** the   **24** a   **25** the   **26** the   **27** the   **28** the   **29** the   **30** the   **31** –   **32** a **33** –   **34** a   **35** –   **36** –   **37** –   **38** the.

Exercise 52 **1** type pitch   **2** daisy-wheel; typestyles   **3** spool   **4** platen   **5** Pica and Elite **6** memory; characters   **7** screens and printers   **8** circular   **9** cassettes and cartridges   **10** Carbon

Exercise 53 **1** (b)   **2** (c)   **3** (c)   **4** (b)   **5** (b)   **6** (a)   **7** (a)   **8** (b)   **9** (c)   **10** (a)   **11** (b) **12** (a)   **13** (a)   **14** (c)   **15** (a)

Exercise 54 **1** are you going to do   **2** am going to copy   **3** going to do   **4** will be   **5** make **6** would take   **7** typed   **8** to finish   **9** used   **10** saw   **11** told   **12** had used **13** would have saved   **14** had done   **15** would have cut   **16** was   **17** to complete   **18** would have been   **19** did she want   **20** need   **21** use   **22** use **23** is   **24** needs   **25** have you ever worked   **26** have prepared   **27** have not operated   **28** is   **29** want   **30** get   **31** go   **32** reproduce   **33** will be wondering   **34** Come   **35** will take   **36** sit   **37** will go

Exercise 55 **1** you ever worked   **2** ever worked   **3** am always using   **4** sometimes type   **5** have often wanted   **6** never seem   **7** usually find   **8** you generally have to be   **9** you ever make   **10** I sometimes do   **11** can usually use   **12** can generally graft **13** I seldom need   **14** are usually

Exercise 56 Letter changes will read: . . . we have opened our new branch at (address). Our representative (name) has now given you the details when he called on you. . . . new centre has allowed us to expand . . . and we now offer . . . present trade discount has been raised from 25% to 33% . . . and we have cut our delivery times from eight to four weeks.

Exercise 57 **1** No, only juniors and trainees under 19   **2** See their managers or supervisors   **3** 1 Jan 19 . .   **4** Help in their careers   **5** No   **6** Only approved courses   **7** The Personnel Manager   **8** A Bank.

Exercise 58 **1** Keep them brief and clear and for urgent communications   **2** 50%   **3** Invoices; credit notes; debit notes etc.   **4** Used only for business, and international calls must be brief and to the point   **5** Correct it   **6** Five times that of ball-point pens **7** No   **8** Safety   **9** Use 2nd. class post   **10** Correcting fluid and grafting **11** Everyone   **12** In bulk   **13** They fell   **14** 35%   **15** Smaller.

Exercise 59   **1** to let   **2** to pay   **3** to give   **4** to get on   **5** to be   **6** to study   **7** to read   **8** to look at   **9** to apply   **10** to get   **11** to go to   **12** to see   **13** to discuss   **14** to be   **15** to make   **16** fill in   **17** to send   **18** to go   **19** to do   **20** to take   **21** to enrol   **22** to contact   **23** to read.

Exercise 60   **1** to make   **2** to use   **3** be   **4** to judge   **5** have   **6** to check   **7** to understand   **8** to cut   **9** to help   **10** to remember   **11** to save   **12** to economise   **13** to think   **14** to put

Exercise 61   **1** along   **2** with   **3** of   **4** from   **5** to   **6** by   **7** into   **8** to   **9** by   **10** with   **11** on   **12** along   **13** to   **14** on   **15** of   **16** for

Exercise 62   **1** contacting   **2** to contact   **3** to phone   **4** write/to write   **5** writing   **6** doing   **7** to get   **8** know   **9** to live   **10** phoning   **11** spending   **12** say   **13** using   **14** to put   **15** to keep   **16** putting   **17** to get   **18** paying   **19** to contact   **20** to call   **21** to pay   **22** calling

Exercise 63   **1** (b)   **2** (a)   **3** (c)   **4** (a)   **5** (c)   **6** (a)   **7** (b)   **8** (b)   **9** (a)   **10** (c)

Exercise 64   (i) 881091
                              6918150
                              RECEIVED ORDER NO 573 CANNOT OFFER BUS WRIT CAT NO 34
                              REPRINTING CANOFFER BUSINESS COMMUNICATIONS CAT A17 AND
                              INCLUDE IN ORDER CNM + ?
                              691850
                              881091
                        (ii) 716813 LAGOS
                              BUSMAC
                              RE IBX ENQUIRY COST FIVE THOUSAND THREE HUNDRED AND TWENTY
                              ONE US DOLLARS LESS 15 0/0 TRADE DISC + +
                              BUSMAC
                              716813 LAGOS
                        (iii) 791013 LONDON
                              HOKMAN 610561
                              DELAY 6 WKS INV NO C1980 DUE TO FACTORY FIRE APOLOGIES
                              GUARANTEE DELIVERY SIX WEEKS FROM PROMISED DATE + +
                              HOKMAN 610561
                              791013 LONDON
                        (iv) We will accept 25 copies of Business Communications Catalogue Number A17
                              (error error) please include this in our Order Number 34 and confirm the trade
                              discount of 33%, repeat 33% Send confirmation.
                        (v) Mr. Chan, our sales manager, will arrive on 20 May at Heathrow Airport, Estimated
                              Time of Arrival (ETA) 08.30. Please confirm his booking for 6 days in the Royal
                              Hotel, and that a representative will meet him.
                        (vi) We accept your quotation for the IBX computer, the *net* price being $4521.00
                              American Dollars (actual price $4521.85, but the odd cents will be left off) if
                              you can deliver within eight weeks or as soon as possible. Our 'Official Order'
                              will follow your confirmation.

Exercise 65   Check list on page 134 for answers

Exercise 66   **1** to remember   **2** to use   **3** to type   **4** to dial   **5** to wait   **6** to do   **7** to let   **8** to give   **9** to contact   **10** to keep   **11** to spend   **12** to make   **13** send

Exercise 67

1 to get **2** to make **3** to find out **4** to save **5** to make **6** to stress **7** to receive **8** to cut **9** to send **10** to save

Exercise 68

1 Yes **2** 50 m.p.g (miles per gallon) **3** De Luxe and LS 1500 **4** LS 850 **5** De Luxe **6** Druse Street **7** Base Road **8** Dock Estate **9** Dean Street **10** 2806.00 **11** 1980 **12** 1800 **13** VII = 7, so there would be 6 other boxes **14** 12.00 **15** (6) so it would be *June*.

Exercise 69

1 June **2** New car registrations in that month **3** December **4** 3000 **5** 4,333⅓ **6** 2000 **7** It's the cheapest model **8** 3000 **9** $2 million **10** Africa and the Mid. East **11** $7 million **12** Commercial **13** 700 **14** $9000 each **15** Dock Estate **16** $5,200 **17** A dotted line **18** Dock Estate

Exercise 70

1 The easiest; the simpler **2** The best; The more complicated; less; the most clear; easier **3** The oldest; the most beautiful; better; earlier **4** clearer; further; less; a wider; the less; the most unusual **5** The most useful; little attention; good order.

Exercise 71

1 The outstanding balance must be paid. **2** We were surprised to receive such an unsatisfactory product. **3** It would be better if valuables were sent by registered post. **4** It is unusual for a company to sell such sub-standard goods. **5** I was surprised when I opened the container. **6** We were surprised to find a cheque had not been sent. **7** I would like to see the manager immediately as I would like to complain about this machine. **8** The delay was caused by the delivery note not being filled in properly.

Exercise 72

1 concerning **2** deliveries **3** consignments **4** delays **5** customers **6** correct **7** future **8** parcels **9** marked **10** check **11** mistakes **12** rely **13** supplier.

Exercise 73

1 to **2** about **3** on **4** For **5** from **6** for **7** between **8** to **9** our **10** in **11** in **12** from **13** to

Exercise 74

1 faded **2** shrunk **3** warped **4** dented **5** smashed **6** wrinkled **7** creased **8** shattered **9** snapped **10** torn **11** strained **12** crushed **13** rusted (oxidised) **14** chipped **15** cracked **16** discoloured **17** knotted **18** loose **19** drenched (saturated) **20** dusty **21** frayed

Exercise 75

1 (b) **2** (c) **3** (b) **4** (a) **5** (b) **6** (c) **7** (a) **8** (b) **9** (a) **10** (b)

Exercise 76

1 03.00 **2** 22.30 – 23.00 **3** 09.30 **4** 02.15 the following day **5** £151.30 **6** No **7** $399.00 **8** £594.81 – £535.33 **9** 22.25, 22.15 **10** 09.35, 11.50 **11** 23.30 **12** 8 hours 12 mins.

Exercise 77

1 details **2** arrangements **3** reservation **4** get **5** terminal **6** bus **7** take-off **8** check in **9** baggage **10** departure **11** called **12** itinerary **13** traveller's cheques **14** bring back **15** visa **16** vaccination **17** reset **18** forward **19** pick it up **20** into **21** available **22** seen to.

Exercise 78

1 Private shower and bath **2** No dogs **3** Parking available **4** No Parking **5** Private telephone **6** TV in all rooms **7** Countryside Hotel **8** Four Star Hotel **9** Sports facilities, sailing, golf, tennis **10** Telex available.

Exercise 79

991453 HK
889160
REFERENCE BKG CAROL DUNN RESVTN 9 TO 16 JUL PLEASE EXTEND TO 23
JUL AND WILL SEND ADDIT DEP $720.00 USD WITH CFMNG LTTR + ?
991453 HK
889160

Exercise 80

889160
991453 HK
C DUNN RESVTN FROM 9 TO 16 JUL EXTENDED TO 23 JUL ON CONDITN ADD
DEP OF $720.00 US SENT BY BK TRNSF WITHIN TWO DAYS REPEAT WITHIN TWO
DAYS
889160
$720.00 TWO DAYS BK TRNSF
991453

Exercise 81

'My name is . . . and I am speaking on behalf of ARC Ltd.'
'. . . would like to hold their annual conference in your hotel on 15 August, and we
will need a room to hold 50 people.'
'. . . from 09.30 to 17.00 . . . supply a four course 'sit down' menu . . . and refreshments
for two breaks. . . . a projector, screen, and sound equipment . . .'
'. . . confirm that the room will be available and offer us a choice of three menus,
and let us know what the tariff covering all expenses for hiring the room, meals,
and equipment will be?'

Exercise 82

1 False   **2** True   **3** True   **4** False   **5** False   **6** True   **7** True   **8** False   **9** False
10 False   **11** True   **12** False   **13** True   **14** True   **15** False

Exercise 83

USSR, Moscow, Rouble; Italy, Milan, Lira; Greece, Salonika, Drachma; Yugoslavia,
Dubrovnik, Dinar; Japan, Kobe, Yen; USA, Washington, Dollar; Germany, Hamburg,
Deutschmark; Norway, Bergen, Krona; Australia, Melbourne, Dollar; Brazil, Rio de
Janeiro, Cruzeiro; India, Calcutta, Rupee; Thailand, Bangkok, Baht; Malaysia, Kuala
Lumpur, Ringgit; Israel, Tel Aviv, Shekel; Canada, Vancouver, Dollar; Jordan, Amman,
Dinar; France, Paris, Franc; Saudi Arabia, Jeddah, Rial; Venezuela, Caracas, Bolivar;
Turkey, Istanbul, Lira.

Exercise 84

1 Switchboard or Receptionist   **2** Switchboard or Receptionist   **3** Continuous
siren   **4** Leave them   **5** To get to know how extinguishers work and where fire
escapes are.

Exercise 85

1 If I saw . . . , I'd get an extinguisher.   **2** If I'd . . . , I'd have reported it.   **3** If I didn't
know . . . , I'd read the instructions on the side of it.   **4** If I am going to . . . , and
it overheats, I'll turn it off.   **5** If I put a fuse . . . , it would cause a fire.   **6** If filing
cabinets are . . . , they topple over.   **7** If a machine is . . . , I should put a note on
it saying 'Do not use'.   **8** If I had broken . . . , I'd have collected the pieces, wrapped
them, and put them in a bin.   **9** Unless a guillotine has a guard, I wouldn't use
it.   **10** If maintenance could not . . . , I'd wait or use another machine.

Exercise 86

1 is   **2** are   **3** have   **4** are   **5** is   **6** hasn't   **7** are   **8** has   **9** have is   **10** are